Small Town Anthology
Volume VII

Entries from the Seventh Annual
Tournament of Writers

Vicksburg Cultural Arts Center

TOURNAMENT
of
writers

A KDP Book
Published by Kindle Direct Publishing

An e-book/Print-on-Demand Publishing unit of
Amazon
410 Terry Ave. North,
Seattle, WA, 98109-5210

www.kdp.amazon.com

KDP is a registered trademark of Amazon.

Copyright © 2021 by the Vicksburg Cultural Arts Center

Edited by J.S. Munson & Syd Bastos

All rights reserved.

KDP Books ISBN 9798466680638

First published in the United States of America by KDP,
an imprint of Amazon, 2021

Vicksburg Cultural Arts Center
PO Box 209
Vicksburg, Michigan 49097
(269) 200-2223

For information on the Tournament of Writers, visit
www.vicksburgarts.com/tournament-of-writers

Dedicated to all the writers out there,
young and old, new and experienced,
who keep at their craft and don't lose sight
of the nature within that compels them
to persevere in the artistic pursuit of storytelling.

"A word after a word after a word is power."
— Margaret Atwood

"Stay faithful to the stories in your head."
— Paula Hawkins

"Writing, to me, is simply thinking through my fingers."
— Isaac Asimov

"If you wait for inspiration to write, you're not a writer, you're a waiter."
— Dan Poynter

"You can't use up creativity. The more you use, the more you have."
— Maya Angelou

"I wrote my first novel because I wanted to read it."
— Toni Morrison

*"Write something that's worth fighting over.
Because that's how you change things. That's how you create art."*
— Jeff Goins

"If you don't see the book you want on the shelf, write it."
— Beverly Cleary

"You can make anything by writing."
— C.S. Lewis

"A book is a dream you hold in your hands."
— Neil Gaiman

"All good writing is swimming under water and holding your breath."
— F. Scott Fitzgerald

"A writer, I think, is someone who pays attention to the world."
— Susan Sontag

TABLE OF CONTENTS

Introduction .... Page 3
What is the Tournament of Writers? .... Page 5
2021 Tournament of Writers Judges .... Page 6
2021 Tournament of Writers Awards .... Page 7

NONFICTION ENTRIES

Ralph Ackley, *The Match* .... Page 13
Carol Braymer, *One Last Date with My Gal* .... Page 15
Mark Giacobone, *Not a Dream* .... Page 18
Sandra Northrup Jones, *It's a Wonderful Life* .... Page 21
Marilyn Jones, *My Blue Bicycle* .... Page 22
Ross Landers, *A Step in the World* .... Page 23
Steve Layne, *Chicago, the Radio and Me* .... Page 26
Mark Lego, *Tribute to Taj Mahal* .... Page 33
Jacob Miller, *The Last Sunrise* .... Page 37
Hayden Moden, *Should Junk Food be Allowed in School?* .... Page 38
Bonnie Oswalt, *A Strange Summer Tale* .... Page 44
Eleanor Ross, *Rebecca Raccoon* .... Page 46
Mark Stucky, *Quantum Acts of Kindness* .... Page 49
Christine Webb, *To Mothers of the Stillborn* .... Page 50

POETRY ENTRIES

Ralph Ackley, *I Am From* .... Page 55
Rhys Biskie, *A Forgotten Battle* .... Page 56
Charles Crouch, *Inhale Exhale (Born & Born Again)* ...... Page 57
Bryon Crowder, *I'll Love You in a Million Ways* .... Page 61
Grace Flanagan, *Lost in No Place* .... Page 63
Ashley Gerber, *Trapped in Anxiety* .... Page 65
Mark Giacabone, *Christmas with My Seven-Year Old* .... Page 67
Maya Grossman, *Joining My Love* .... Page 70

Marilyn Jones, *A Cute Little Visitor* ....Page 71
Sandra Jean Northrup Jones, *Dragonflies Dance* ....Page 72
Sydney Kaiser, *Ethereal* ....Page 73
Tracy Klinesteker, *I'm So Sad* ....Page 74
Ross Landers, *End of the Crucible* ....Page 75
Hannah Laughery, *America's True Horror Story* ....Page 77
Mark Lego, *A Salute to Our Soldiers* ....Page 79
Stephanie Lewman, *Hope* ....Page 80
Jacob Miller, *Asphodel* ....Page 81
RJ Robertson-DeGraaff, *Trees Had Souls* ....Page 82
Lillian Ross, *Oh We Wish* ....Page 83
Finnegan Ross, *Summer* ....Page 84
Eleanor Ross, *Scotland* ....Page 85
Ailia Shaak, *Between* ....Page 86
Mark Stucky, *Broken Beauty* ....Page 93
Christine Webb, *Hope* ....Page 94

FICTION ENTRIES
Ralph Ackley, *The Escape* ....Page 97
Grace Flanagan, *The Life of a Priceless Pen* ....Page 101
Mark Giacabone, *Crouching Tiger* ....Page 104
Katie Grossman, *The Treat* ....Page 105
Marilyn Jones, *She Gave it a Try* ....Page 107
Hannah Laughery, *As Fate Would Have It* ....Page 110
Sky Lester, *Just a Moment* ....Page 117
Hayden Moden, *Valley Forge* ....Page 123
Jacob Miller, *The Stowaway* ....Page 124
Finnegan Ross, *Dragon Diaries* ....Page 128
Lillian Ross, *Tweety's Diary* ....Page 130
Christine Webb, *Alone Together* ....Page 136

Acknowledgements ....Page 143

Introduction

I wonder what an archeologist or a scholarly graduate student would think if they found this anthology a century from now. Would they see facets of their own lives reflected in the creative writing featured in this latest volume of the Small Town Anthology series? I predict that they would recognize some timeless themes in the following pages, but that they could also uncover some topics reflecting concerns specific to our own time. What can we learn about ourselves in these pages written in 2020 and 2021?

In Small Town Anthology, Volume VII, you will find pieces by new writers and seasoned writers of all ages and walks of life. Many of these works discuss timeless themes such as longing for love, losing love, and disappointment in love. The classic theme of military life—from a memoir about joining the marines, to a poem about the daily grit of marching, to a poetic celebration of our soldiers—shows our community's respect and honor for sacrifice. Following in the Romantic poet tradition, the anthology includes many close-up images and introspection about the natural world, featuring dragonflies, hummingbirds, encounters with bears, pet racoons, and some memorable cats!

If we dig deeper, though, we can see some topics and ideas that feel like they are responses to the effects of a lingering pandemic. Interestingly, not one of the submissions mentions Covid-19. Many of the stories and poems are memoirs, retreats to the romantic past, or philosophical ponderings about the cycle of life. We find our community either escaping to the past or fantasy, or tackling the pandemic by thinking about the big patterns of birth, growth, wisdom, and death.

Our youngest writers, seem to be our most nostalgic, writing with a sweet longing about distant lands and lost loves. Our young adult writers tackle the big questions, many of them thinking along the lines of the title "Lost in No Place." You will find in this anthology many stories about people who were stuck or lost. "Why are you lost?" asks a wise woman in one of the poems. Our youth also tackle difficult current social issues, such as human trafficking—a nightmare that also depicts being stuck and trapped. Many of our adult writers turned their pens to the topic of family legacy and created crisp and vivid journeys back to simpler times.

As you encounter these works, I hope you will appreciate the technical skill of our writers. Many of them know how to guide their readers toward an expectation, only to give them an enjoyable twist they weren't expecting. Many of them also give their readers a surprise dose of hope at the end of their poems and stories. We may be somewhat stuck in 2021, but hope still permeates our community. One of our poets describes hope as "the frosting in the middle of a twinkie." Enjoy that sweetness as you walk through the back roads in Small Town Anthology VII.

Now, it is an honor to present, on behalf of the Vicksburg Cultural Arts Center, the Seventh Edition of the Small Town Anthology! Whether a prize-winner or not, every entry is included in this book. Thank you to every writer represented, for taking the time, making the effort, and summoning the courage to present your works to the public. We appreciate your talent and wisdom.

Alisha Siebers, Executive Director of Vicksburg Cultural Arts Center
September 2021 - Vicksburg, MI

What is the *Tournament of Writers*?

The Tournament of Writers encourages and promotes our local writers with a competition that is open to residents of all ages in Kalamazoo County and in its surrounding counties. In addition to celebrating writers with cash prizes, the competition also provides constructive and encouraging feedback from judges to help participants gain insights from thoughtful readers.

This competition accepts submissions in the genres of poetry, fiction, and nonfiction.

Each piece is received and presented to a panel of judges who score the submissions using a rubric that evaluates effective use of language, correct grammar and usage, powerful deployment of literary techniques, and creativity. Based on these scores, judges award prizes within each genre, separated out by the following age divisions:

Youth: through 8th grade

Young Adult: 9th grade through 25 years

Adult: 26 through 50 years

Senior: 51 years and older

From all of the top winners of all divisions and genres, the Judges' Choice Grand Prize Winner wins the entire Tournament.

Every entry received for the Tournament of Writers is published in our annual "Small Town Anthology" book, which is available for purchase through our website. We conclude the Tournament each Fall with a book signing party to celebrate the courage and creativity of our local writers.

Tournament of Writers 2021 Judges

Kristina Powers Aubry

Aaron Behr

Coralee Behr

Leigh Fryling

Kitty Martin

Jake Munson

Alisha Siebers

Melissa Sparks

Katherine Suender

Don Wiertella

2021 Award Winners - Nonfiction

First Place

Junior Division: Eleanor Ross
Rebecca Raccoon

Young Adult Division: Jacob Miller
The Last Sunrise

Adult Division: Christine Webb
To Mothers of the Stillborn

Senior Division: Carol Braymer
One Last Date with My Gal

Second Place

Junior Division: Hayden Moden
Should Junk Food be Allowed in Schools?

Adult Division: Ross Landers
A Step in the World

Senior Division: Bonnie Oswalt
A Strange Summer Tale

Third Place

Senior Division: Steve Layne
Chicago, the Radio and Me

2021 Award Winners - Poetry

First Place

Junior Division: Lillian Ross
Oh We Wish

Young Adult: Sydney Kaiser
Ethereal

Adult Division: Ross Landers
End of the Crucible

Senior Division: Mark Stucky
Broken Beauty

Second Place

Junior Division: Ashley Gerber
Trapped in Anxiety

Young Adult: Hannah Laughery
America's True Horror Story

Adult Division: Christine Webb
Hope

Senior Division: Ralph Ackley
I Am From

Third Place

Junior Division: Rhys Biskie
A Forgotten Battle

Young Adult: Jacob Miller
Asphodel

Adult Division: Stephanie Lewman
Hope

Senior Division: Charles Crouch
Inhale Exhale (Born & Born Again)

2021 Award Winners - Fiction

First Place

Junior Division: Hayden Moden
Valley Forge

Young Adult Division: Sky Lester
Just a Moment

Adult Division: Christine Webb
Alone Together

Senior Division: Ralph Ackley
The Escape

Second Place

Junior Division: Lillian Ross
Tweety's Diary

Young Adult: Grace Flanagan
The Life of a Priceless Pen

Adult Division: Katie Grossman
The Treat

Senior Division: Marilyn Jones
She Gave It a Try

Third Place

Junior Division: Finnegan Ross
Dragon Diaries

Young Adult: Hannah Laughery
As Fate Would Have It

Senior Division: Mark Giacobone
Crouching Tiger

Judges Choice Grand Prize Winner*

To Mothers of the Stillborn

Christine Webb – Adult Nonfiction

Featured on Page 50

*Chosen by Judges from top winners in 2021.

NONFICTION

The Match
Ralph Ackley
Senior Division

I remember watching him in the receding light of a cold winter's night, just after he found out he had colon cancer. Warming himself by the wood stove, he picked his teeth with a wooden match, a habit he had developed over the years as there never seemed to be any toothpicks around, or so he said. Mum teased him that he never took the time to look for them. He usually replied that he thought she was purposely hiding them. He was used to having wooden matches in the front pocket of his jeans, especially during the winter months when he would be cutting firewood back behind the old homestead where he grew up. The leftover matches he used to build a small fire to warm himself around lunch time provided the makeshift toothpicks.

The light of the fire glowed around his face, reflecting the stove's features in his eyes. I wondered, as I stared at him, if he was remembering the one match he had left that had proved to have a more important use than picking one's teeth one summer day, years before he had ever come down with the dreaded disease. As he stared ahead into the fading sun setting across the bay, was he thinking of that early summer fishing trip our family had taken with the Makers? Our two families did everything together, sleepovers, family picnics, and weekend camping trips.

That particular weekend, we gathered all of our gear, loaded up the Cocoa Express (his 'customized 1970 Ford Bronco with dual wheels fit with heavy chains in the back) and headed out to East Stream, back underneath a small ledge called Cocoa Mountain. I remember that morning we had split off into two groups. Dad's brother-in-law Burton, my cousin Greg and I headed with the fishing gear (homemade poles made from alder branches fit with fishing line, old hooks, and a can of freshly dug worms) toward Wheeler Heath. Our hearts beat in anticipation as the light of an early dawn crept slowly to the east. We had hoped to creep up quietly on the brook trout that lazily rose from beneath the still waters of Bagley Brook meandering through the heath lying below the aged spruce.

As always, it was hard going, stepping over the myriad mounds of swaths of grass that lay like a carton of eggs all around us. We had to walk gingerly or we would quickly sink back into surprisingly deep water, run-offs from the main stream we were heading to. Mum, Dad, Aunt Joyce and the younger kids stayed back while we headed north east of the camp. A good 600 yards separated us. We hadn't even wet our lines when we heard a yell behind us.

"We're going over there!" Dad hollered.

Burton yelled back, "Over here! The fish are over here!"

At least that's how we heard the conversation. Later, we learned something quite different was shouted out. What Dad had actually said to us was:

"Bear over here!"

We thought they were going to try another location. All we could do was wave for them to come to where we were as we had immediately started getting significant bites on our lines. From where we stood plying the waters of Wheeler Heath, we never saw a thing. A sow had apparently caught wind of our human scent and, in trying to protect her young from what she perceived to be a threat, she began loping her way toward them with surprising speed! She was used to traversing the heath. This was her domain, not ours!

Everybody in Dad's party started running toward us. At one point he slowed down to pick up our cousin Tony who had fallen trying to jump the grassy mounds with his little five-year old legs. Just before bending down to swoop him up, Dad reached into his jean pocket to pull out a wooden match. He lit it on his front zipper and threw it toward the bear. We hadn't had much rain that spring and the field was incredibly dry. The heath lit up right away and the wind drove the flames rapidly toward the old sow. She retreated quickly with her brood but the fire spread like crazy! Dad and the others caught up to where we were and told us the whole story. We couldn't believe our ears! We hadn't seen any bears. Evidently, she had been hidden from view and became part of the backdrop of an island of fir trees to the west.

For a while longer, we fished up and down the stream, keeping our eyes on the growing fire to our left. Finally, we decided we had better get back to camp and report the fire as it was fanning out all along the heath and up into several stands of hardwood, splintering the dry forest like fresh kindling and leaving smoldering patches of ground all around. It took some time for us to believe a bear had actually chased Dad and his crew but we knew he'd never had set fire to anything without a good reason. He told the truth to the fire warden. He had told him that he had set the fire to protect his family and friends.

No charges of arson were ever levied against Dad. He was even paid for helping to fight the fire that ended up burning over 75 acres of grassland and forest. He may have killed a few trees, but he had saved a life, perhaps several lives. Practically the entire town of Cutler understood that and told him that they would have done the same thing. Maybe. Maybe not. Perhaps others would have panicked. Still fewer would have thought to look into the pockets of their jeans for a single match that "just happened to be there" and light it off their zipper.

I looked at him as he continued to gaze into the waning flames of the woodstove's fire. I wondered silently "Was his heart full of fear before he fumbled for that match? Did he act on instinct? Did he share the frightening nightmares of a bear chasing them that my mother and brother had weeks later experienced? How did it impact him to think about how he has saved a life?" I'm sure he was grateful.

He never spoke much of the incident but I'm sure that he thought about it a lot. Maybe reminiscing about such things helped him deal with any lingering regrets, the kind of regrets that are normal for somebody thinking about the cancer eating away at him, ready to snuff out too quickly a life well-lived. Maybe he was grateful that he had not picked his teeth that morning.

One Last Date with My Gal

Carol Braymer
1st Place, Senior Division

He woke to strange sounds. What was going on? "Where the hell am I?" he asked himself. Then he remembered the fall and breaking his hip. And now he was stuck in rehab, when all he wanted was to return to his house on Sunset Lake and have life return to normal.

The early mornings were the worst, he thought. They routinely woke him early to check his vitals, then he would lie awake, unable to return to sleep. How long had they been here he wondered? Three weeks maybe? Give or take a few days that sounded about right. All the days were the same so it was hard to keep track. Blood pressure and oxygen level checked, medications adjusted, physical therapy, being wheeled down to the cafeteria for yet another meal of cold coffee and even colder eggs, and more naps than he could imagine.

Things had really gone downhill quickly. One fall, that's all it had taken, he thought. One fall and a broken hip and their lives were changed forever. She had been here before with pneumonia, and even though they said she had recovered, she had been readmitted the day after he had gotten here from the hospital. She was the thing that kept him going, his bride of 73 years. She was the reason, he felt, he had lived so long. He had to take care of her. And now they were both here.

He rang for the aide to help transport him to the bathroom and settled in for the wait. "You have to call for them well ahead of when you actually have to go because they sure take their time coming to help you" he muttered to himself. "But when you're ninety-eight and you break your hip, you're at their mercy." He thought of her, wondering if she was awake yet, hoping she was still asleep. She needed her rest if she was going to recover this time. She had always been so small and feminine, he remembered, and he'd always wanted to take care of her. He thought back to when they first met.

"I'm so excited to go to the USO dance tonight. Our white dresses with the red boleros really look sharp, and are perfect for Valentine's Day." Betty *had recently turned eighteen, and was now allowed to date. The Valentine's Day USO dance would be the perfect place to meet Navy men.*

They met at the dance, and were attracted to each other right away. "Would you like to dance?" Betty had asked. "I don't know how" he had replied. "Well, can you roller skate?" she asked. "If you can skate you can dance." He had been nervous about making a fool of himself, but he learned to dance that night.

Since he had a car, he drove Betty and her friend home when the dance ended. Betty later admitted she had arranged things so she was sitting next to him in the front seat. That way he'd have to drop her off last. They spent as much time together as possible before he had to leave for the South Pacific. They sent letters, and even talked about marriage. But she hadn't wanted to end up a war widow with a child if anything were to happen to him, so they continued to get to know each other better through their letters. In August of 1945, while he was on leave, they asked her brother to help them elope. He declined, saying he was afraid of their mother's wrath. Fortunately, her other brother helped them, and they ran off to get married.

Thinking back on those early days made him smile. They had lived a full and happy life together. They had raised four great kids, had traveled, had vacationed in Florida during the winters and enjoyed boating in Michigan in the summers. A man couldn't have asked for a better mate, he told himself. They had invested time and energy in their home and family, but also in their relationship. And today he was going to have a "date" with his gal. The staff was going to wheel them down to a private room so they could have lunch together. God, how he missed their house at the lake, waking up with her next to him, and enjoying each other's company. But seeing her today was just what he needed to lift up his spirits.

"Betty, you look so pretty today!" the nurse exclaimed. "And is that a new blouse?" Betty beamed. "Yes!" she replied. "I'm having lunch with my husband today, and I want to look my best. We've been married for seventy-three years, and spent almost every day together, so having both of us in here in separate rooms, and now separate buildings, has been hard."

"Well let me help you into the wheelchair and I'll have an aide push you over to lunch. We don't want to keep your date waiting" teased the nurse.

An aide came and pushed Betty through the building to the walkway. Along the way nurses and aides commented how pretty Betty looked today. Her *hair was done nicely and she had applied a bit of makeup. She was obviously excited to see her beau again.*

Lunch with her had been wonderful, he thought. Just what the doctor ordered. She looked so pretty today. She had always been a beautiful woman, but today she looked radiant. She always stressed that they should make an effort to look their best, and today she had achieved that. I'll have to work harder to recover so we can go home together, he thought. The food that had been served was good for a change, and he had enjoyed it. As their son was wheeling her out to take her back to her room, she had taken his hand and said "I love you Don." And he had replied "I love you Betty." Now he was going to take a rest so he could work hard tomorrow in physical therapy.

A short time later his son returned to his room. "She's gone Pop" he said through his tears. "We got back to her room and her heart just stopped. She slipped away peacefully."
They had prepared for this moment, had known it would be coming soon, but he had always thought he would go first. At least I was there until the end to take care of her, he thought. He was surprised his own heart could keep beating when she, who was such a part of him, was no longer of this earth. He knew he had difficult decisions to make about just giving up and following her or trying to accept there was still beauty in the world and enjoy whatever life he had left. He was thankful she had gone peacefully with no pain, and in the arms of her son. But at that moment, with the pain of her passing still washing over him, he was most thankful he had been given one last date with his gal.

Author's Note:

The morning after Betty passed away Don insisted he be brought home to their cottage on Sunset Lake. He struggled without Betty, and spent many hours talking to her. He told me one day that he had decided he didn't want to continue without her, but that she wasn't happy with that decision. So he was going to enjoy the beauty at the lake, and had a goal of living to be one hundred. Sadly, he did not reach that goal. Just five months after his beloved Betty died, Don also passed away peacefully. Up until the end he frequently talked about how the memory of that last date with Betty helped him cope with her passing.

Not a Dream
Mark Giacabone
Senior Division

I was about three years old, walking barefoot (and alone) in my grandparents' front yard when I stepped on a burr. With prickly needles stuck to my big toe I sat down and began crying, knowing that my life had just been destroyed.

With a tear-soaked face and blurry vision, I looked up to see my grandmother slowly approaching out of nowhere.

She walked with a slow lumbering gait, unaware of the pending emergency.

Without speaking she miraculously pulled the burr from my toe and helped me stand up.

Fast forward 25 years and I found myself in another life rut.

Frustrated and unable to figure it out, I just kept spinning my wheels.

One night while sleeping, my rapid eye movement was interrupted.

My (then passed) grandmother was approaching again.

With soulful eyes she looked at me as if to say….. "What now Marko?"

Grandmothers are like that.

It's a Wonderful Life
Sandra Jean Northrup Jones
Senior Division

What if...

What if...my Grandpa Davis didn't go watch the recital where my Grandma danced.

What if...my Grandpa didn't follow her back home to Ohio and give her a Rose.

What if...my Grandpa and Grandma didn't have my Mom, their fourth child.

What if...my Mom didn't meet my Dad at an insurance office.

What if...my Mom and Dad didn't have me, their third child.

What if...I didn't meet my husband, Bob after a softball game in Vicksburg.

What if...Bob and I didn't have two daughters, Casey and Carlee.

What if...my daughters didn't have children, my grandchildren. What if...

It's a "What If" Life

It's a Wonderful Life

Fate
Ancestry
Teach
Enjoy

My Blue Bicycle
Marilyn Jones
Senior Division

In 1908, my dad's father was killed in an industrial accident. His mother had several children to raise by herself. Since her husband had a brother and sister-in-law who were childless, she gave her baby, Roy, to John and Anna Clark. My mom and dad were married at age 18 and were divorced when I was a baby, so I never really knew him.

I lived with my maternal grandparents in a small, humble home and I was happy there. For one week each summer, Grandma and Grandpa Clark, as I called them, took me to their big farm house. They had a touring car, a big box telephone on the wall and two upright pianos in the parlor. To me, I thought they were rich. All year they had saved the Sunday comics and I spent hours reclining in the hammock, reading the Katzenjammer Kids, Alley Oop, Tillie the Toiler, Little Annie Rooney and Henry.

I was used to helping with the laundry and ironing at a young age. I did the dusting and swept the spider webs down in the outhouse. For that entire week, I had no chores. Grandpa had chicken and cows. Each day, he and the Collie dog went down the lane and drove the cows back to the barn. Barefooted, I liked walking on the warm cow-patties that were dried from the sun. He milked the cows by hand, sometimes squirting milk at the barn cats that licked their whiskers and enjoyed the treat. Grandma made pancakes for our breakfast each day, as large as a dinner plate. I never figured out how she flipped them.

Each night I slept on a scratchy couch in the parlor. The walls were covered with large photos of long-dead ancestors. It seemed to me that we had a thunderstorm every night. I would curl up in a ball and cover my head. Each time the lightning would brighten up the room, all those eyes were staring at me. I never told anyone how scared I was.

My dad was a salesman in Chicago and would drive down on the Sunday that I was there. Grandma was up at dawn, preparing chickens, baking pies and husking corn. It would be a lavish feast. At home we usually had boiled potatoes and codfish gravy, which I thought was delicious. Each year, I hoped that my dad would tell me that I was pretty, but he just commented on how much I had grown.

One year, my dad brought a new wife, Dorothy. She was very nice but it ended my hopes that my folks would get together again. The next year, they had a darling baby. Barbara-Ann was my half-sister and I was delighted. I never saw her again and have often wondered what kind of a life she had and if she knew about me. I later heard that Dorothy got a divorce and she and Barbara-Ann moved to Texas. He was later married and had more children.

Roy was supposed to pay child support for me, but it was depression years and nobody had money to spare. By now, I lived with my mother in a drab, furnished room in Detroit. She struggled to support me as a cocktail waitress in a beer garden. She was happy when Roy would mail a $5.00 bill. She opened a savings account in my name in the Detroit Post Office. It grew to the huge sum of $35.00.

I had never received a birthday or Christmas gift from my dad, not even a card. I was amazed when he sent me a note that he was sending me a gift that would be delivered. I couldn't imagine what it might be. A large carton arrived and it contained a large, shiny, blue girl's bicycle! I had never dreamed of having anything so wonderful. I learned to ride it between the streetcar tracks on the busy streets of Detroit.

Since our room was on a 3rd floor walk-up, the landlady said that I could keep the bike in the vestibule under the stairs. That was a good place, until one day it wasn't there! After telling the landlady that my bike had been stolen, she informed me that she had locked it in the cellar until my mother paid her back rent.

I didn't know that Mom was looking for another place to live. She found a vacant room in the next block. The landlady always went to the local theatre on Sunday afternoon when the price was twelve cents and each patron was given a dish of pink Depression glass.

We had about two hours to make our getaway. All of our clothes were in two old cardboard suitcases and our other meager belongings were thrown into a dishpan and a large waste basket. Away we traipsed down the sidewalk.

There was one more thing… my bike. Time was running out! Mom brought a hammer and pounded the lock off the cellar door. The light was dim and I floundered around in cobwebs until I found it in the coal bin. It wasn't easy dragging it out and up the steps, but finally we were out in the open and we hurried down the street, leaving the rent bill unpaid.

That bike had some great rides when I was in High School. As an adult, I rode it to work, the grocery store, the library and even to church. It also took me to my grandson's Little League games.

In 2009, I took a bad fall... not on the bike; I tripped on a step. The doctor said that I wouldn't have recuperated as well if I hadn't been in good physical shape from my bike riding.

I'm thankful that my Dad loved me enough to give me one of the best gifts that I ever received.

A Step in the World
Ross Landers
Adult Division

I didn't do so well in High School. I wasn't a delinquent or anything. I was a good boy. I just didn't do my homework or study. I had better things to do, like play video games, watch movies, and think about cute girls. My senior year I didn't even realize I had to get my act together until my girlfriend at the time, Nikki, asked me, "You really aren't preparing for college?"

"Should I be?" I responded.

She dumped me promptly. A week before prom too. That's ok. She was half-Chinese, half-Japanese, but her personality was one hundred percent Americana. Too spicy for me. She saved me the money I would have spent to rent a limo. We rode my buddy's minivan into prom instead.

There was another girl my heart belonged to anyway. Jen. Had I done something a little different, she and I would have been long since married and had a family and all that. The girl who got away. The girl who embedded herself in my brain to the point that to this day I still think of her from time to time. I haven't seen or talked to her since I left.

I had no future and girls were driving me nuts. On top of that, Sammamish became too expensive to live in unless you were some fancy pants tech guru or something like that. I knew how to turn on a computer, search for lewd anime pictures, and had rudimentary HTML skills. That's about it. The rising social media websites and programs like Dreamweaver made my HTML knowledge obsolete.

I'd managed to get into Bellevue Community College, but I didn't have any direction. I failed out of classes and dropped others. My dad paid the bill. He wasn't happy. "If you aren't going to go to school," my dad said, "then you better find a job or join the military!" Unbeknownst to him and me, one of those things was about to come true.

My dad was a pilot. My mom was too. It's funny how my two younger siblings and I have no taste for aviation. The act of it anyway. When I was young my dad was the private pilot for a big shot Japanese CEO. He made trips all over the world and frequently visited Japan. His tales of Tokyo, Osaka, Sapporo, and other Japanese cities must have resonated with me at an early age. When I hit thirteen years I was captivated with Japanese culture. I was born in Florida and my dad had a good friend from Florida whose son also fell into the otaku lifestyle.

"There must have been something in the water down there in Florida," my dad said after he caught me watching *Sailor Moon*.

Maybe that is the reason. Whatever the case is, I loved anime, I loved Japan, and I wanted to get the hell out of Sammamish.

My best friend, Brian, might have also been an influence of things that were to come. He was younger than me by a month, but because he started school in California, he was a grade ahead of me. While I was still a senior in high school, he went off to Prague to teach English. By "teach English", I mean party like crazy. He came back from Europe as the party master with countless wild stories of his exploits. Though I don't have a single partying fiber in my body, Brian's tales of far off lands and exotic peoples served to increase my appetite for travel.

I'd landed a job at the Issaquah Barnes and Noble, which I've heard has been closed since I left. (Amazon consumes all.) I worked as a cashier, customer service rep, and stocking boy. When I finally gave up on college entirely, I figured I'd just work at Barnes and Noble forever. But the things I mentioned earlier weighed heavy on me.

It started at Barnes and Noble. I wore a wrinkled polo shirt, wrinkled khakis, and old scuffed up, dirt ridden tennis shoes. My brown hair was a grease covered messy mop plopped on my head. I manned the information booth. It was slow. If you've ever worked a customer service job, you know you just can't stand there idly even if you have nothing to do. I took it upon myself to pretend to dust the map section shelves.

I must have looked like I hated life when he showed up.

He was a tall skinny man. He wore jeans and a normal long-sleeved shirt with a baseball cap on his dome. There was an energy about him of raw, pure confidence.

"How can I help you?" I asked as I stopped pretending to dust the shelves.

"Could you help me find a book called *Game of Thrones*?" Keep in mind, this is 2004, many years before HBO's *Game of Thrones* would become a household name.

"Yeah, it's right this way."

I led him to the Fantasy/Sci-Fi section and took him to the M's (for Martin). I pulled the paperback novel from the shelf and handed it to him. "There you go," I said.

"Thanks," he replied, "Hey, you mind if I ask you a few questions?"

Weird.

"Sure?"

"You in school?"

"No."

"Why not?"

"Just need some time to figure things out."

"You ever think about joining the military?"

I had. Let's rewind a bit. I had several supervisors at Barnes and Noble. I don't remember any of them except Paul. Paul was a skinny, cigarette smoking, energetic old man. He once told me, "I only read Sci-Fi and military history." I think I latched onto him because he was one of the few employees at Barnes and Noble who weren't hippies. He'd also been in the Marine Corps. He'd done the full twenty, had been a drill instructor, and had been stationed in Japan. Even married a Japanese woman. I liked listening to his stories. I asked him once, "What was boot camp like?"

"You know the movie Full Metal Jacket?"

"Yeah."

"Like that, but 100 times worse."

One time, I was mulling over the idea of joining the military at my mom's place and she said, "Join the Air Force. Whatever you do, don't join the Marines."

Life is kind of funny.

Back in the Fantasy/Sci-Fi section, the man said, "The reason I ask is because I'm the Marine Corps recruiter for the area."

He handed me his card. Staff Sergeant Smith. "Think about it and if you are interested, give me a call."

That's really all it took. The business card in my hand was like a key to a doorway leading me out of my dead-end life. I called later and scheduled a meeting at the armed service recruiting center just down the street from the community college.

Smith wore his dress blue Charlies. His blue trousers bore the blood stripe down the side of each leg. A beige belt with a gold buckle wrapped around his waist where his crisp beige shirt was tucked. The top button of his shirt was undone revealing a white shirt underneath. His ribbons were proudly displayed on his left breast. The rank of Staff Sergeant shown on the side of each short sleeve.

He sat me down at a table and took out a bag filled with dog tag-like flash cards. Each tag had a word on it like responsibility, purpose, adventure, and comradery. He told me to organize them from what was most important to me to least important. I don't remember the order. Looking back on it I don't think the order mattered. I remember just chatting with him like we were long time buddies. I told him about my thirst for adventure and getting out of my current situation.

"Can you guys send me to Japan?"

"No promises, but it's possible. We have bases there."

Good enough answer for me.

I'll be real with you; I didn't want to go infantry. That's basically how I put it to Smith. Anything but infantry. Look, I love my infantry brethren. They are amongst the smartest, funniest, and most badass people I've ever met in my life. But I didn't want to get shot at.

Smith suggested military intelligence. I was down. But when he asked if anyone in my family was from a different country, I mentioned that my stepmom was from Scotland. I guess that doesn't fly in military intelligence. Got to watch out for those Scots! Smith then suggested avionics. I thought this was neat. Maybe I didn't have the nerve to be a pilot, but I could continue the family's legacy in aviation through working on flight electronics.

Looking back at it, I'm pretty sure someone having a stepmom from Scotland doesn't disqualify them for military intelligence. Smith probably just had an avionics quota he had to meet. Doesn't matter. If I placed high enough on the ASVAB I could join up in avionics!

I don't remember the time between that meeting and when I took the ASVAB. But I did eventually take it. I remember guessing on most of the questions. There was no way Smith was going to send me through avionics. I was a dummy. Still am in some regards. Later that day Smith called me up and said I did great and that I qualified for avionics. Like I said, I think there was a quota to meet.

He told me the next step was the medical check and I had to do it bright and early the next day at the MEPS center in downtown Seattle. A room was reserved for me at the Holiday Inn across the street from the MEPS and Smith drove me in. I never stayed in a hotel room by myself up until that point. Nerves and excitement prevented me from getting much sleep.

The next morning there were a bunch of boys present for the health check. It was a whole day event. We went from station to station where a doctor inspected a different aspect of our bodies. I don't remember many of the details, but some tests stuck out, like the famously named "duck walk" where we started at one side of the room and had to walk across the room in a crouched position. And then there was the prostate check. I walked into a small office, where a doctor in a comically cliché white lab coat told me to face away from him, drop my pants, bend over, and spread my cheeks. Nothing went in, but the doc took a nice long look. Ask any Marine about the prostate check and they'll get a chuckle over it.

By the time the health check ended it was 5 or 6 in the afternoon. Everyone was tired. They had us wait in a lobby for a good while before someone came out and said, "It is time to swear in!"

Was this really it? Was I really doing this? I didn't want to put everything I did for the health check to waste so I figured why not? Let's just jump in the water!

We all went into a room that had a podium and the American flag. We all stood in organized intervals from each other. A man stood at the podium and told us to raise our right hands. We did. Then he told us to repeat after him. We did. We gave the oath. I'd be lying to you if I said I remember the exact words. What it comes down to is we swore loyalty to America, that we'd protect it, and die for it if we had to. Then we signed the documents. I was in the delayed entry program which meant I wasn't shipped off right away. This marked my time as a poolee. I had 5 months to tie up loose ends and get my body ready for bootcamp.

Smith met me outside the building. He congratulated me, gave me a packet, and a videotape that gave me some idea as to what to expect. Nothing can really prepare you though. He also gave me a Marine Corps sticker and a grey shirt that had an image of the Marines raising the flag on top of Mount Suribachi. Under the Marines was written "The Few. The Proud."

Smith drove me back to my mom's. He told me he'd see me later at the pool function and drove off. My family was out. The condo was empty. I threw my clothes off, turned on the shower, and got in. While the hot water poured over me, the realization set in. I bounced up and down. I screamed with excitement. I'd finally taken a step forward into the world. I turned off the shower, got out, put on some boxers, and donned the new Marine shirt. Exhausted, I plopped down into my bed and fell asleep.

My mom woke me up an hour or two later and saw the shirt. "What did you do?" Her eyes were wide with disbelief.

Well, I sure didn't join the Air Force.

"I swore in. I'm shipping off for Marine boot camp in 5 months." She cried.

When I told Paul the next day at work, he patted me on the shoulder and said, "Oorah." I'd hear and say that slogan many times over the next couple of years.

I told Jen, hoping to score some points with her. Her dad had been in the Army in his youth and maybe me going into the Marines would impress her. If it did, I couldn't tell. She wasn't cold to me or anything. She was just normal. We were friends, which is what drove me nuts. If you ever fall in love with a girl who is your friend, be up front with them and if the relationship doesn't evolve, walk away. It's better for both parties.

Brian didn't like it. He was a more peace-and-love kind of guy. This is where a rift between him and I began to grow, and that gap would never close again.

My dad was proud, but uncertain. He knew me for the lazy, aloof, unathletic boy that I was. I couldn't get through community college. How was I supposed to get through the Marine Corps? It was an understandable concern.

My mom, though she had been scared at first, believed in me and filled me with courage.

The next step was the pool functions held at the recruiting station every week. Smith was tasked with the daunting mission of getting my gamer-boy body ready for MCRD San Diego. Even though the pool functions would be but a sample of bootcamp, they would prove to be my first test in my path of becoming a United States Marine.

Chicago, the Radio and Me
Steve Layne
3rd Place, Senior Division

I grew up fifteen miles south of Kalamazoo, Michigan. Anyone who knows his geography realizes that Kalamazoo is almost exactly half-way between Chicago and Detroit on I-94. People living in this area are torn in their loyalties between the two larger cities. You are either a Tigers fan or a Cubs/White Sox fan. You root for the Lions or you root for the Bears. You love the University of Michigan Wolverines and hate the Notre Dame Fighting Irish or vice versa. You love the Bad Boy Pistons or you love Michael Jordan. It is rare to be a fan of both Detroit and Chicago.

In the early sixties, I was close to becoming a teenager. I had been enamored by popular music since I was a kid, listening to my parents' recordings of Frank Sinatra, Johnny Mathis, Andy Williams, Tony Bennett and a lot of Country & Western. I learned to appreciate this music in later life, but I did indeed hear it at an early age.

Also buried in that collection were albums by Elvis Presley and Ricky Nelson. I could relate to these guys in a much stronger way than I could to the Ray Conniff Singers or Mitch Miller. I soon discovered that I wanted to start my own record collection, reflecting my own musical tastes. It wasn't long before I had purchased my first album, "Tie Me Kangaroo Down, Sport" by Rolf Harris and my first two singles, "Devil in Disguise" by Elvis and "Ally Ally Oxen Free" by the Kingston Trio, all in 1963.

Of course, the Beatles changed everything in late 1963 and early 1964. Their first appearance on the Ed Sullivan Show in February 1964 was the biggest event in my young life, as it was for millions of teens throughout the world. I loved them and by extension, I fell in love with the radio that played their hits. The remainder of my teen years revolved around rock & roll music.

In the early Sixties, my grandfather had given me an old 1940's-vintage Zenith tube radio. I would turn it on, wait for the dial light to begin to glow, and suddenly the world opened up to me. I would listen as soon as I got home from school or late at night after everyone else in my family was asleep. This was the vehicle that led me to the wonderful world of rock and pop music.

One of the obvious attractions of listening to the radio was everything Motown. The airwaves were saturated with music from the Motor City. Motown had started out as a local independent label, but quickly became a national force. How could you not love the Supremes, Temptations, Four Tops, Smokey Robinson, Stevie Wonder, Marvin Gaye and all the others? This led to a larger focus on Detroit area artists such as Bob Seger ("East Side Story," "Heavy Music"), the Rationals ("Gave my Love," "Respect") and later, SRC, The Stooges and the MC5.

While most of my friends concentrated on the east side of Michigan for new sounds, I was listening in a different direction. My grandfather's radio allowed me to hear how Chicago rocked the Sixties.

In listening to my radio late at night, I was able to pick up strong signals from all over the country, including WABC in New York (Cousin Brucie). But the stations that I consistently came back to were WLS and WCFL, both 50,000 watt juggernauts out of Chicago. In addition to hearing the national hits that I could also hear on Kalamazoo stations, such as WTPS, WYYY or WKMI, I also encountered a number of local Chicago bands that did not necessarily make the national charts.

I still remember the DJs - Dex Card, Larry Lujack, Art Roberts, Clark Weber, Bob Sirott and Ron Riley on WLS; Joel Sebastion, Ron Britain and Dick Biondi on WCLF. Biondi was also later on WLS. I especially loved Dex Card (and later Larry Lujack), who ran down WLS' Silver Dollar Survey every week. The survey ranked the listed top 40 hits plus a number of records "bubbling outside". You could hear all of the national hits, but what was exciting was hearing a number of Chicago-area bands that you could not hear anywhere else.

These bands all started out as garage bands signed to local independent labels such as USA, Centaur, Dunwich and Destination. It would take a local hit or two before the national labels such as Columbia and Mercury rushed to sign these bands. At the time, I wasn't necessarily aware that these bands were from Chicago, but I did recognize the fact that I was not hearing most of these songs on Kalamazoo radio.

The DJs at both WLS and WFCL were instrumental in the success of these local groups. The bands would be heavily promoted by the radio stations, who sponsored sock hops, battle of the bands and personal appearances by the groups. It was very common to hear "Join me, Ron Britain, at the Cellar in Arlington Heights to present the Cryan' Shames this Friday night."

This type of promotion intertwined the radio stations and the local artist, resulting in huge popularity for both the bands and the DJs.

One of the first Chicago groups I remember hearing was the Shadows of Knight out of Arlington Heights, doing their version of Them's "Gloria." The band was influenced by the Rolling Stones, the Yardbirds and American R&B. They later had a semi-hit with a cover of Bo Diddley's "Oh, Yeah" before fading into obscurity.

At approximately the same time, the Cryan' Shames released their version of "Sugar and Spice," previously recorded by England's Searchers. The band was known for creating great melodies and harmonies with strong group songwriting, especially by guitarist Jim Fairs and bassist Lenny Kerley. In addition, the band featured percussionist J.D. Hooke, who was missing a left hand (thus his stage name).

Among their other local hits was "I Wanna Meet You," "Mr. Reliable," "It Could be We're in Love," "First Train to California" and "Greenburg, Glickstein, Charles, David Smith and Jones." Unlike some local bands, they also received positive reviews for a couple of LPs, "A Scratch in the Sky" and "Synthesis." Their music sounds just as fresh today as it did in 1967.

In a similar vein, The New Colony Six had a number of Chicagoland hits in the mid-to-late Sixties. The group started out with a garage band sound and evolved into more of a ballad and bubblegum band. Their first release in 1965 was a punk-sounding "I Confess." The band's early stage attire was very similar to the outfits worn by Paul Revere and the Raiders, another garage band from the Pacific Northwest. The Raiders reached much greater heights than the New Colony Six, but coincidentally the two groups lived in the same duplex in Los Angeles for a time in the mid-Sixties.

Other New Colony Six records hitting the Chicago charts in this time period were "Love you so Much," "I will Always Think About You," which actually got some national exposure and resulted in a national tour with the Beach Boys, and "Things I'd Like to Say." The group played into the early Seventies before disbanding.

The biggest, most well-known band of the Chicago scene in the Sixties was the Buckinghams, from the northwest suburbs. Starting with "Kind of a Drag," released on USA records, the Buckinghams (originally the

Pulsations) were quickly grabbed by Columbia records and proceeded to get national exposure with "Don't you Care," "Hey Baby (They're Playing our Song)," "Mercy, Mercy, Mercy," "Susan" and "Back in Love Again." The Buckinghams were as hot as anyone in 1967-68.

Other Chicago-area groups on the Windy City charts during this time included the Ides of March (pre-"Vehicle") with "You Wouldn't Listen to Me," the American Breed with "Bend Me, Shape Me" and "Step out of Your Mind" and Michael and the Messengers with "Romeo and Juliet." There were other groups who never made the charts or even won a recording contract but there was an undeniable plethora of talent in Chicago in the mid-Sixties.

As noted, the majority of Sixties Chicago music was released on independent labels, severely limiting national exposure. That limited exposure did not stop one Kalamazoo kid from enjoying this great music. I owe a great debt of gratitude to WLS, WCFL and my grandfather for giving me that old Zenith.

Thanks Grandpa.

Taj Mahal (My Bengal Cat)
Mark Lego
Senior Division

I woke up in the morning, on a typical spring day. This would be no ordinary day, but one that will not be forgotten. I heard the sound of a cat's cry. It was my beloved Bengal cat, Taj Mahal. What's a matter, girl?

Only yesterday she was a happy, beautiful and seemingly healthy feline. Now, she was lying on the porch, in great agony. Her rear legs seemed to be paralyzed, and she was barely able to move at all. She was in dire misery. Panic set in. I rushed to make a phone call for advice. My mind raced as I tried to decide the best option. After moments of anxiety, I realized that she would need to be put to sleep, much to my dismay and regret. As I figured out where I should take her, I wrapped her in my fleece jacket and placed her in the passenger's side of the truck. I was dreading the drive that I didn't want to take but we hurried off on this grim journey.

She laid there, her eyes so bright, with her loving face, forsaken by her ailing body, laboring to breathe, uttering periodic meows of suffering. Knowing the inevitable result, I wished she could stop hurting. As we drove on, there would be moments of silence and rest. Suddenly, she would rise up so full of life, then the reality of the haunting meows of pain. How much longer before we get there? A little while yet. Then another brief period of silence. The minutes seemed to pass like hours. We're almost there, I said to my sweet, loving cat. One more time she sprung to life, as if to say a farewell to the life that we had shared. And then back to silence again.

In all the confusion, I drove past the place we needed to go. I had to go down and turn around and deal with more traffic. Finally, we got to the destination. As I picked up her limp body, I realized that she had passed on. Tears of sadness filled my eyes, for she was really gone. Yet, there was a relief in the fact that she was no longer suffering and that her loving spirit was finally set free.

Afterward, I thought that at least she didn't die in some strange place. She knew I was there with her in the end. With a heavy heart, I could return home with her, and give her a goodbye that she so deserved. I placed her to rest in the yard that she loved to frolic in and enjoyed so much. She was a truly unique cat that will be sincerely missed. I treasure the time and the memories which have enriched my life. Days like these are a bold reminder of how precious and fleeting Life truly is.

The Last Sunrise
Jacob Miller
1st Place, Young Adult Division

(An excerpt from a larger work)

Characters

HARRY TRUMAN: 33rd President of the United States who took over command of the war after Roosevelt died.

EMPEROR HIROHITO: 124th Emperor of Japan.

RICHARD NELSON: Radio operator for the *Enola Gay*. Earlier scene is based on letters written by William Kinnaird.

PAUL TIBBETS: Pilot of the *Enola Gay*.

ROBERT LEWIS: Co-pilot of the *Enola Gay*.

THOMAS FEREBEE: Bombardier of the *Enola Gay*.

THEODORE VAN KIRK: Navigator for the *Enola Gay*.

(*TRUMAN, HIROHITO, NELSON, LEWIS, TIBBETS, KIRK, and FEREBEE enter. TRUMAN and HIROHITO stand on opposite ends of the stage while the others stand center.*)

TRUMAN. (*Addressing Hirohito*) Emperor Hirohito, by the power vested in me by the United States of America, I ask you for your complete surrender: call back your forces, lay down your arms and hand over control of your government to us. We can end this war tonight; no more blood needs to be spilled.

HIROHITO. And allow my country and people to be subjugated by the gluttony of the American government, to be treated like second-class citizens in their own country? You know what my answer is President Truman.

TRUMAN. (*A sigh, pause, then turning to address the bombers.*) Then it is with great reluctance that I authorize the use of the atomic bomb. We have given the Japanese an opportunity for peace, but no agreement could be made. End this war.

(*The bombers salute. Sound of an airplane can be heard.*)

LEWIS. Monday, 2:45 AM, August 6th, 1945.

NELSON. The Enola Gay took off from Tinian Island.

KIRK. Currently 2,526 kilometers from our target.

FEREBEE. Carrying 9,700 pounds of explosives, nicknamed "Little Boy."

TIBBETS. Operation Centerboard I: transport the atomic bomb to Hiroshima and drop it on the city.

(*a beat*)

TIBBETS. Anything on the radar, Van Kirk?

KIRK. Nothing, sir.

TIBBETS. Keep an eye on it. Our mission hinges on not encountering enemy aircraft.

KIRK. Yes, sir.

TIBBETS. How's the bomb looking, Ferebee?

FEREBEE. It's secured, sir.

TIBBETS. How's she handling, Lewis?

LEWIS. She's dragging a little, but that's to be expected. Stripping her of the turrets and plating sure helps keep it balanced.

TIBBETS. Anything from HQ?

NELSON. Nothing, sir. 2,000 kilometers.

(*a beat*)

NELSON. Sir?

TIBBETS. What is it, Nelson?

NELSON. Sir, do you really think this is a good idea?

LEWIS. These are our orders.

FEREBEE. The Japs need to pay for Pearl Harbor.

NELSON. But, sir–

TIBBETS. –And more importantly, this will end the war faster than any amount of men could.

NELSON. Yes, I know, sir, but–

TIBBETS. –But nothing, Nelson.

(*roughly ten seconds of silence*)

KIRK. 1,000 kilometers.

(*Tibbets takes out his watch, looks at it and puts it back.*)

TIBBETS. We should get there around 8 am.

FEREBEE. I hope they give us some time off when we get back. Even just a nap.

LEWIS. A cold beer.

FEREBEE. And none of that oriental shit! I am talking about a nice Budweiser.

TIBBETS. You like that shit, Ferebee?

FEREBEE. Hell yes, sir. It's all I ever drank growing up.

NELSON. Sir?

TIBBETS. You're not going to tell us you also like Budweiser, are you?

NELSON. No, sir. I am just wondering what the population of Hiroshima is like.

TIBBETS. You were in the same briefing room as the rest of us, Nelson.

NELSON. I know, sir, but I saw you talking with General Spaatz before we took off. I was wondering if he said anything to you about the city.

TIBBETS. Officially, the target is a military base. But it does have a small civilian population of somewhere between 200,000 and 300,000.

NELSON. Small?!?

KIRK. 500 kilometers.

NELSON. Sir, that is not a small population. That's a–

TIBBETS. –That's enough, Nelson.

FEREBEE. Why do you even care? They're just Japs.

NELSON. They're people, Ferebee. Just like us.

FEREBEE. No, not like us. The Japs bombed us when we had our pants around our ankles, stumbling around. No one with *honor* does that.

NELSON. But we have no idea what this bomb will do.

TIBBETS. Nelson.

KIRK. 100 kilometers.

FEREBEE. Who cares what happens to them?

NELSON. I do! These are innocent people!

TIBBETS. Nelson!

NELSON. I cannot sit idly by and watch while we drop this bomb!

TIBBETS. (*Tibbets' hand goes to his pistol.*) You wanted to see action, did you not, Nelson? Well, this is it.

KIRK. 10 kilometers

(a beat)

TIBBETS. Prime the bomb.

FEREBEE. Yes, sir.

(*Ferebee makes a motion to prime the bomb.*)

LEWIS. Beginning our descent.

(*They all react slightly as the plane begins to decrease in altitude.*)

KIRK. Less than 1 kilometer.

TIBBETS. When it is in your sights, drop it.

NELSON. Colonel, this is wrong. This bomb will kill thousands of people.

TIBBETS. We are soldiers. Soldiers do not question orders. You will do your duty, soldier.

FEREBEE. Yes, sir.

(*Ferebee motions for releasing the bomb, either a handle or button. They all react as 10,000 pounds is released from the plane. 10-15 seconds of silence from when the bomb is dropped to when it lands. Light cue of light orange/yellow from the blast.*)

NELSON. What have we done?

(*Tibbets looks at his watch.*)

TIBBETS. At approximately 8:15 AM, the first atomic bomb exploded. Targeted eliminated.

NELSON. What have we done?

(*The bombers exit.*)

TRUMAN. The world will note that the first atomic bomb was dropped on Hiroshima. We have used it in order to shorten the agony of war, in order to save the lives of thousands and thousands of young Americans–

HIROHITO. –And what about Japanese lives?!? You killed over 50,000 Japanese citizens–

TRUMAN. –It was a military base–

HIROHITO. –with just one bomb!

TRUMAN. This was payback for Pearl Harbor.

HIROHITO. Payback? There is a difference between killing 2000 soldiers and eradicating tens of thousands of civilians!

TRUMAN. We are not the ones who started this war.

HIROHITO. No, you were not. But you have ended it in such a way you can never undo.

(*Exit Hirohito.*)

TRUMAN. (*A sigh, addresses the audience.*) And we shall continue to use the atomic bomb until we completely destroy Japan's power to make war. Only a Japanese surrender will stop us.

(*Exit Truman.*)

Should Junk Food be Allowed in School?
Hayden Moden
2nd Place, Junior Division

Imagine, it's snack time at school, and you pull out some sliced Granny Smiths to graze on. You happily munch on its soury sweetness while you watch the others pull out potato chips and Fruit by the Foots. You wonder why they are having junk food at 9 in the morning, but you mind your own business. Later on in the day, you see them tired and very unenergetic. You wonder what is wrong with them. How come they aren't their usual, energetic, peppy selves? Then you remember the unhealthy foods they had for a snack. Does that contribute to the problem? Yes, it does. Having junk food in schools results in lower energy levels and slower learning in the classroom. It also leads to pupils being more at risk for diseases such as diabetes and obesity. In my opinion, junk food should not be allowed in schools.

Junk Food in Schools Results in Lower Academic and Athletic Performance

One of the main reasons that many children have a low academic performance in class is because of their junk food consumption. Many studies have facts to back this statement. For instance, on the website www.wilder.org, it states that: "Research suggests that diets high in trans and saturated fats can negatively impact learning and memory. Nutritional deficiencies early in life can affect the cognitive development of school-aged children. And access to nutrition improves students' cognition, concentration, and energy levels." The diet of a student also results in athletic performance. Another website called www.hss.edu states that eating junk food results in too many fat calories and not enough carbohydrates. This then reduces protein and energy. This can rapidly decrease sports performance in many students.

An Unhealthy Diet Can Result in Diabetes and Childhood Obesity

If junk food is a huge part of your diet, you could be at risk for diseases such as diabetes and childhood obesity. Diabetes is the condition in which the body does not properly process food for use as energy. Most of the food we eat is turned into glucose, or sugar, for our bodies to use for energy. The pancreas, an organ that lies near the stomach, makes a hormone called insulin to help glucose get into the cells of our bodies. If your pancreas cannot produce insulin, you can become very sick. This is the main reason for this illness, and studies show that eating fat foods is a big contributor to diabetes. The website www.nutrition.org.uk informs people that; "Dietary factors can contribute to the development of type 2 diabetes. The most significant factors are a diet high in energy, fat (especially saturated) and low in fiber. This kind of diet is harmful because it can cause weight gain and also impairs insulin action." Another disease that can be caused by consuming too much food that is bad for you is childhood obesity. The website www.ncbi.nih.gov says: "The increased consumption of more energy-dense, nutrient-poor foods with high levels of sugar and saturated fats, combined with reduced physical activity, have led to high obesity rates among children." Do you want your children to be plagued with one of these diseases? I sure don't.

Well, now I'll think twice the next time I pop a potato chip in my mouth. I believe junk food should not be allowed in schools for many reasons. Eating such unhealthy foods can result in lower academic and athletic performance, and it can result in childhood obesity and diabetes. It is worse enough when people eat too much unhealthy foods at home, but now they can eat it at school as well? Schools should provide a healthy and balanced meal and should monitor what the kids are eating. Now I'm not saying to not indulge yourself every once in a while with a good ice cream sundae, but be sensible. Balance your diet with healthy foods and protein. Then maybe, just maybe, not so many kids will face such horrible tragedies in the not so distant future.

A Strange Summer Tale
Bonnie Oswalt
2nd Place, Senior Division

When I was growing up, most of the months of July, August and into September were spent at our family camp in Canada.

My father had severe allergies and asthma. After years of searching in the Western states, he "heard" that the Eastern shore of Lake Superior was where he might escape his summer plague, and a plague it was.

As a young man in Detroit, due to his allergies and asthma, he would often be carried by stretcher to the Detroit River docks and put on a Northbound freighter, returning in several weeks, much improved.

In the early 1930s, my father and a college friend camped along the Batchawana Bay on the eastern Canadian shore of Lake Superior. The bay is protected by several islands from the often-stormy Great Lake. He did find his health much better, and the following summer, he and his new bride, my mother, purchased property along the Batchawana River and Bay in Ontario. This location had been a lumber camp in the late 1800s and had several old log cabins remaining.

By 1935, my parents began to build a log home, preserving two of the original old dwellings as potential guest accommodations.

This new property proved to be the ideal place for my allergy/asthma burdened father. It became a labor of love to turn this old lumber camp into their summer haven which we, in later years, named "Awana Batch."

By this time, my father was retired, had a reliable manager for our dairy farm, and was ready to breathe the refreshing air and enjoy this beautiful spot.

Our small hometown was an hour north of Detroit. My parents were very civic-minded and active in both communities and were very excited about their new Canadian retreat. Consequently, they each invited any and all to come North and spend a week with our family; however, except for relatives or very close friends, few made the long Northern journey.

It certainly was a long excursion. In the 1930s and 40s there were no superhighways, no Mackinaw or International Bridge. It was a good two-day trip, two ferry boat rides, border customs, grocery shopping, and then a two-hour drive North on a gravel, winding road along the Canadian Lake Superior shore. Few but family made the trip.

One summer, late afternoon, we were startled to hear a car come down our long wooded drive and begin tooting their horn. A man, woman and young girl climbed out and excitedly yelled, "Hello! We are finally here!"

With their arrival, a very interesting week followed.

My parents were well known for their gracious hospitality. We children were instructed to be the same and to treat everyone like family. So we all hurried out of our cabin and warmly welcomed the new arrivals.

They were great guests. They loved to play games, enjoyed hours of boat rides, fishing and swimming, and raved about my mother's cooking, done in those days on a woodstove. They settled comfortably into one of the old lumber camp cabins, enjoying our hospitality!

During this week, I noticed my parents discretely huddling. They had no idea who these people were! We were too polite to ask, and they certainly seemed to know us!

As I look back some seventy-plus years later, I think what a different time it was. It was a safer, gentler time. It was a kinder time.

They, the mystery family, may have been professional vacation crashers. I'll never know. But I do know "they" had a lovely all-inclusive vacation and we, in turn, enjoyed their companionship.

My family still loves "Awana Batch." It is a special spot that many of our friends have visited. Both of my parents are gone, and I don't believe they ever solved the identity of the mystery family. That particular week has become part of our family "lore."

It truly made a strange summer to remember.

Rebecca Raccoon
Eleanor Ross
1st Place, Junior Division

When you think of raccoons, you barely ever think of them as being part of the White House. But in 1926, Rebecca, a raccoon, was brought to the White House to be served at Thanksgiving dinner. Yuck! Who serves raccoons for Thanksgiving dinner!? President Calvin Coolidge and First Lady Grace Coolidge decided to keep Rebecca as a pet instead and let her live at the White House with them. I would have chosen to keep her as a pet, too!

Sometimes Rebecca liked to do mischievous things. She unscrewed light bulbs and pulled plants out of their pots. She was on a leash outside but she could roam free in the house. Sometimes they put her in a bathtub with a little bit of water and a bar of soap and she would play with it for a long time. Some people thought she was a magician because she would wriggle out of harnesses and chew through cages with wooden bars. If I were a raccoon living in the White House, I would probably look for trash cans, climb trees, dig holes, and chase around any animals on the White House lawn. I would probably not listen to the White House Staff or Secret Service.

They built a house for Rebecca outside with a wire fence for safety. The house was made of wood. It was located on the South lawn, right outside of the President's office. I bet that President Coolidge liked to watch Rebecca play while he was working!

Rebecca even went on vacation! She went to South Dakota's Black Hills for 3 months. She traveled there by railroad with the Coolidges. Rebecca would break out of her cage and climb the highest pine tree behind the summer White House. And she would annoy the Secret Service by playing keep away for a couple hours. If I were a raccoon, I would have loved to play tricks on the Secret Service!

Soon Rebecca got a raccoon friend called Reuben. It would have been cool if they had baby raccoons, but really they didn't get along. Reuben escaped a lot and eventually ran away without a trace. Rebecca also started escaping a little bit more, probably running through the city looking for trash cans! Soon the Coolidges donated her to the zoo, and she died a few weeks after moving to the zoo.

Quantum Acts of Kindness
Mark Stucky
Senior Division

Our universe collectively consists of tiny acts, as innumerable particles in indeterminate positions fluctuate randomly. Einstein thought there must be order and meaning, a Theory of Everything, behind the seeming chaos in the quantum realm, a vast realm of subatomic scale that forms the fabric of the cosmos.

Our social fabric also consists of tiny acts, acts of love and kindness. A mother nurses her newborn, a nurse holds the hand of a dying patient, and all small acts of loving kindness in between weave together the random events in our lives.

A quantum Theory of Everything eluded Einstein. But an acts-of-kindness Theory of Everything for each of us is:

- Love God with all your heart and soul and strength and mind.
- Love people of all religions, races, genders, and other identities.
- Love your neighbor as yourself.
- Love your enemies.

Kindness theory is easy. Practice is hard.

But acts of not-so-random kindness construct and change our world.

To Mothers of the Stillborn
Christine Webb
1st Place, Adult Division
Judges Choice Winner

Welcome to the sisterhood.

I'd say I'm glad you're here, but I'm not. I wish you weren't. I wish I weren't here either, yet, as my husband always says, "It is what it is."

Put your stuff down; make yourself at home. You're going to be here a while...forever, really. You can't *ever* leave, no matter how many nights you stay up crying and wishing you weren't in the sisterhood. But no matter! Since you're new, there are some things you should know. Follow me - I'll show you around and give you the grand tour.

You may notice our soundtrack playing in the background. It's sad music that sounds quaint considering all we've been through. All those artists who sing about heartbreak and strum away their chords of woe? They seem laughable now. What do they know of heartbreak?

We know heartbreak. Heartbreak is holding your dead baby. When he looks straight through you with glassy eyes that will never see your face, and you wrap his tiny (too tiny) hand around your finger? *That's* heartbreak. Leaving the hospital with empty arms is heartbreak. Discussing funeral arrangements and answering questions like whether or not your infant son will be cremated is heartbreak.

The most heartbreaking moment for me was when I lay in my hospital bed, in extreme physical and emotional pain, and I turned to see my husband. He was holding our small baby, rocking him back and forth, back and forth, as if he could soothe him. My husband cried silently, as if tears could bring him back to life. He would have been such a good father. He *was* a good father, if only for a few precious moments.

Pop songs can't touch what we know of a broken heart.

Here's our supply closet. You can come here when you run out of Kleenexes. The day after my sweet Charles died, I walked around aimlessly with a roll of toilet paper because I had no Kleenex. I would rip off a few squares, soak them in tears and snot, then throw them...wherever. It didn't particularly matter where. Not a lot matters on the day after your son dies. So don't be like me - there's plenty of Kleenex in the supply closet. Don't go through toilet paper like you've got indigestion.

Here's the living room. You get to choose a couch, and you'd better make it a comfy one. You're going to be spending a lot of time on your couch in the next few weeks. I'd say I laid on the couch and watched Netflix, but I didn't. I laid on the couch and stared at a screen without absorbing anything that was going on. I might as well have been staring at the wall (and I did my fair share of that too). It was like someone unplugged the world - nothing continued. I didn't work, I barely slept, I soaked rolls of my crypaper...I had no plans except to survive, and even that was a chore on most days. My body felt painfully empty and simultaneously full of lead. Most things felt impossible. I still remember the first day I got out of sweats and put on real pants. That was my huge accomplishment of the day - I put on pants, and I thought I deserved a medal.

Over here you'll see our whiteboard of "Stupid things people say." There's not anything great to say in these circumstances, mind you, but some people say things that are exceptionally stupid. We in the sisterhood have a running list and vote for each other's to see who's heard the dumbest stuff. Here, you should vote for mine. I added the one that says, "Your son had your nose? That's probably why he died...he didn't want to live life with that nose. Ha ha." and "We thought we were losing our baby at one point. Obviously, we didn't because our son is fine, but I know *just* how you feel."

Remember - they are trying to help. You'll say that to yourself hundreds of times in the upcoming weeks: *they're just trying to help.* Try to see the intention instead of the words they use. It's like you have to have x-ray vision for speech. I wish we had goggles to offer you to help you see through the words. We've got scientists working on it.

Here's the bathroom. The mirror is kind of large, but you probably want to avoid looking into it. On most days, my face looks foreign - like someone drained the joy out of my eyes and the color from my cheeks. My hair sticks up at weird angles, and I try really hard to care, but I come up short most of the time. It's best just to avoid the mirror.

The bathtub is another tough place. One well-wisher sent a variety pack of designer bath bombs (who knew there were designer bath bombs?), and I've spent several nights in the bath, trying to grasp at any level of calm. Instead, I see my flat stomach and am filled with white-hot hatred for the body that couldn't protect my son.

It's not only the death of our children that makes this so hard, sister. It's the death of our dreams, our futures, and our legacies. There was so much left undone when these tiny souls left the world, and now we'll never know what they could have become.

Don't look at me like that. I know it looks scary. It *is* scary. It's terrible. But come over here. I have more to show you.

This is the kitchen. Please notice that the oven burners are completely clean. The oven looks brand new. That's because we never use it. In the first month after my son died, I didn't cook for myself once. Meals kept showing up out of nowhere - people from church, people from school, friends, family...somehow it all got coordinated, and the meals kept showing up. Groceries appeared in my refrigerator because someone would bring them over. Every meal felt like a hug. When people didn't know what to say, they offered casseroles, brownies, or even a store-bought pizza. I counted my thank-you cards when I sent them out: thirty-nine. I wrote thirty-nine thank-you cards to people who cared for us after Charlie was born. I cried and smiled as I wrote them.

Here in the garden, we have flowers people sent. In the weeks after Charlie died, my kitchen and dining room looked like a greenhouse. There were plants and flowers everywhere. Some of them are still alive weeks later.

I never knew how many people cared about me until my son died.

I can't call it a silver lining - there's no silver lining when your child dies. But I will say that people are the reason you will survive the awful first few weeks. I would have forgotten to eat. There seemed to be no reason to smile, but I did smile when the florist kept making deliveries - the poor guy had to drive down our super long and bumpy driveway three times on one day, and his truck may never recover.

You won't be okay at first, sister, but you'll survive. As you keep surviving one day and then the next, no matter how insurmountable they seem, you'll find yourself slowly crawling out of the darkness into something that resembles a normal life. I'm a little new here myself, to be honest, so we can help each other learn to navigate the sisterhood that neither one of us wanted to join.

POETRY

I Am From
Ralph Ackley
1st Place, Senior Division

I am from black spruce lined along
clam shell driveways;
perfumed lilacs below the bank
and the gnarly, old tamarack
stretching and yawning above Grampa's fields

I am from Mamma's boiled dinners and
Saturday night baked bean suppers
her yeast rolls rising in the oven and homemade bread
fresh cole slaw, red hot dogs (only in Maine) smothered with ketchup
and rhubarb custard pie for dessert

I'm from "rise and shine!" Sunday mornings
bacon sizzling, eggs frying over-easy
fresh brewed coffee percolating
steamy odors wafting through the kitchen
then curling their way upstairs to my bedroom

I am from Dad's King Edward cigar clenched between his front teeth,
one gold filling glinting in the sun and oily smells of engine work
from grease beneath my fingernails and our backs along the cold, concrete floor
turning a wrench and synching a screw
on that pretty, aquamarine Dodge Monaco, 1972

I'm from "Cut the crap or I'm comin' up there and I'll pound your liver!"
From "your feet are gonna get cold if you don't put
an extra pair of socks on lemonhead!"
and "we'll do some fishing when you get home from school"
(hen scratches of a short note from home, 1983);

I am from Elmer Look and Frances Preston lines
from his brother Ralph and Lulu Huntley's too;
twelve children on both sides (Mum and Dad were kissing cousins)
dozens of aunts and uncles and big Sunday gatherings
and kids playing until fading summer sunlight

I'm from Tumble's course, goat hair
From Uncle Neal's unshaven stubble
and the smell of Bugle Boy tobacco ---
cigarettes he rolled by hand
From sister Joan's stringy, knotted hair and
Grammy's wrinkled, time weathered face

I am from these memories
Cascading downward and
fading now as the years rush by;
a leaf still attached
To the deeply rooted tree

A Forgotten Battle
Rhys King Biskie
3rd Place, Junior Division

A mountainside rocky and rough

Long ago tall and tough

Now battered and broken with cracks on the side

Now battered and broken with cracks one foot wide

With nails in its rocks holding swords and shields

With cracks and dents like old empty fields

From battles long ago now forgotten and past

Just like that mountainside forgotten and sad

Inhale Exhale (Born & Born Again)
Charles Crouch
3rd Place, Senior Division

Mother:
She is the wellspring
Of your life.

You emerge
From within
That soothing security,
That loving comfort
Of your Mother's
Body.

Your blood,
Your bone,
Your flesh,
Your body
Is of her body.

Now disconnected,
Separated,
You cry,
You wail
At your profound loss.

You Inhale!

From that moment
Of your new life,
Though separated
In the flesh,

Your Mother
Will remain
Your refuge,
Your fortress of healing
To soothe
Your hurt,
Your pain,
Your suffering.

And she will be
Your Joshua's Horn,
Trumpeting your successes,
And extolling your virtues
To the world
In resounding
Celebration;
And crumbling
The self-imposed walls
Of your own insecurities,
Your uncertainties,
Your fears.

And as your
Own life
Blossoms,
As you grow
Into your
Own body
And find your way
In life;

Still,
Still you will seek
To reconnect
To your Mother,
To be soothed,
To be comforted,
To be instilled
With hopefulness
Within the refuge
Of her love.

For nothing
Of this Earth,
Nothing of the flesh,
Or of the Human Spirit,
Connects you to your
Own life,
As does your
Mother.

And when that
Day arrives,
As it will
For you,
As it does
For us all,
And your
Mother,
For the very
Last time:

Exhales!

You will cry,
And you will wail
Once again
For your
Profound loss;
Just as you did
As a child
Born of a new life.

And indeed,
There will be
New Life,
For your
Mother's
Human Spirit
Will be Reborn
Into God's Kingdom;
And she will become
A Child of God!

And when
Your tears
Have lessened,
You can rejoice
And celebrate
Your Mother's
New Life.

And in the days
That follow,
When you
Require refuge,
When you seek
Comfort,
And healing,
Just close your
Eyes
And imagine
Yourself
Held within
Your Mother's arms,
And immersed
Within your
Mother's Love.

And if you
Remain still,
And strong
In your belief,
I am certain
You will hear
The Trumpeting
Of Joshua's Horn.

I'll Love You in a Million Ways
Bryon Crowder
Senior Division

Last Night
I dreamed an amazing dream
That you were the field
And I was the tree
And I said unto you:
I love you in a million ways!
You warmly smiled back at me, and said:
I know .... I know!
I'll hold you tight
Ev'ry day
And ev'ry night
And I'll never let you go
Said I:
When the summer sun burns hot
I'll cast shade
Upon your face
And I'll deflect
The angry storms
That try
To take you away
Each spring
I'll set
A million leaves
Each leaf
A small love letter

In autumn
I'll paint them
All pretty colors
The prettier
The better
And come fall
I'll send them unto you
One by one
And
Two by two
Until I have told you
I love you!
In a million ways!
For all my time
And
For all my days

Lost in No Place
Grace Flanagan
Young Adult Division

The sun's rays are cold
on the face of grounded bird,
for wings unused grow mold
leaving dreams blurred.

Who will weigh the last breath?
And tell me this is only hypnotism?
My hands stained like Lady Macbeth,
and this a violent schism.

I've shattered society's code,
leaving me to wander
on the self-condemning crossroad
enjoined forever in dishonor.

The sun is the squanderer
of warmth upon his face,
yet he flaps into arms of conjurer,
away from golden embrace.

So we find ourselves in No Place.
Where the laughing teacher schools
us to our memories erase,
leaving us emotionless fools.

But the images refuse to burn
in bonfires of intensity,
and still the bird yearns
despite blackness's density.

An entire lack of empathy
is present in my wake
and my insolent identity
does nothing for the bird's sake.

Tipping time adds to our ache
and the bird sings in pain
forcing me awake
to mend my soul slain.

But my soul is permanently
bloodstained and my memories in dejection
leaving my soul dark and drained.
Murder ravaged my introspection.

Trapped in Anxiety
Ashley Gerber
2nd Place, Junior Division

Trapped under the surface
The pressure beating my eardrums down
At this point, I'm in too deep
I feel as though I'm going to drown

It seems as though the air to breathe
Is oh so far away
Too hard to break the surface
Murky, dark, and grey

My lungs
Deprived of air
My flesh
Discolored flair

My heart
It's racing
Beating hard
Pacing

Back and forth
Within my chest
My thoughts replaced
By nothingness

My vision fades
All blue and blurry
Numb am I
Consumed by worry

But someday
I will break the surface
Breathe the air
And find my purpose

Someday I'll rise
Above the ocean
All my troubles
Left unspoken

Someday I'll see
A different view
Someday I'll see
The world like you

Christmas with My Seven-Year Old
Mark Giacabone
Senior Division

T'was the night before Christmas, and all through the house
Not a creature was stirring, not even a mouse

The stockings were hung on the living room floor
With backpacks and shoes stacked up by the door

With a TV remote nestled right on her lap
My wife settled down for a long winters nap

Camille rushed to the sink and she brushed up her teeth
She was ready for bed and ready to sleep

She gave me a hug with wonder and bliss
And then on my cheek, a butterfly kiss

She said "Daddy I love you" and she started to snore
And I quietly turned and I crept out the door

I walked down the stairway, I walked down the hall
I looked out the window and watched the snow fall

The moon reflected on the snow frozen hard
It covered the junk I left out in the yard

When suddenly, to my surprise, there rose such a clatter
And I sprang to my feet to see what was the matter

I heard someone shout, I heard someone squeal
And I knew right away, it must be Camille

I ran up the stairway as quick as a flash
I tripped on a pop can and fell on my arm.

I burst into her room all worried and bleak
And then she sat up and started to speak

She said "Daddy, I have a question and I need you to listen"
"Could you please explain the Social Security System?"

I had to think quickly inside of my mind
for Social Security easily defined

I said "Camille, they take money, money you've earned"
"And then when you're older, the money's returned"

"And, to keep the system smooth and never encumbered"
"Everyone gets their own nine-digit number"

"No need to be worried, no need to be miffed"
"When you're an old lady, Social Security won't exist"

"Now you can be happy from your head to your feet"
"So, why don't you lay down and just go back to sleep?"

Blessed are the children who sleep through the night
But Camille, she was up for a late evening fight

It was no longer cute, it was no longer fun
When she said "What if your Social Security number is…..one?"

"I can't answer your question" I tried to explain
"I don't have the numbers and I don't know the names"

"To be perfectly honest, my sweet little chum"
"Nobody has just… the number one".

"BUT WHAT IF THEY DID?" She started to yell
And I knew right away this would be a tough sell

"BUT WHAT IF THEY DID?" she loudly demanded?
"But nobody would" …. I politely commanded

She repeated the question, it was always the same
She snapped and she growled and she called me by name

Camille is determined, steadfast and true
When she wants your opinion, she'll give it to you

Santa was flying from the north to the south
Camille was at home, foaming at the mouth.

Hurricane Camille, the words are synonymous
I was looking online for Parents Anonymous

The road rage continued, it was now getting late
"What we've got here… is a failure to communicate"

Well, I ran out of words and I ran out of luck
I threw in the towel, and I finally gave up

She heard me exclaim as I stormed out of sight
"PLEASE GO TO SLEEP…..(It's been one hell of a night)"

Joining My Love
Maya Grossman
Junior Division

I sit upon this soaring swing, thinking
About your eyes, how they twinkle and glow
Like the moon in the deepest nights, sinking.
You may have been broken but did not show,
There is an engulfing feeling of woe
When your name is mentioned I quickly hide.
You were my treasure and to whom I owe
My life to my savior my joy and pride.

I may pass due to this sadness inside
She possessed my love day in and day out.
I do not think I can set this aside,
For she put a hole in my heart, no doubt.
If I pass do not shed one single tear,
For I will be with her, you shall not fear.

A Cute Little Visitor
Marilyn Jones
Senior Division

I bought a hummingbird feeder
And hung it out on my porch one day,
To entice them with some sugar water
And hoped they would fly my way.

Many hours are spent on my glider
Right now, I was reading a book,
I hadn't seen any birds there yet
You have to be quick, but I happened to look.

And there he was, with a pretty read throat
Happy to find some lunch right here,
He slurped it up with his straw-like beak
I sat very still, it had nothing to fear.

He flapped his tiny wings so fast
They quivered in a blur,
It excited me to observe nature
And this unique happening to occur.

Wasn't it clever of that little bird
To find it and hover, in mid-air?
I was in awe of God's little critter
Until it pooped on my chair!

Dragonflies Dance
Sandra Jean Northrup Jones
Senior Division

Love to watch Dragonflies' Dance

So...quick & elegant moves

Hovering like a Helicopter

Free to float in the air.

Turning a sharp right

Up then down and all around

Surprise landing on my knee

Two together...silly smile

Ethereal
Sydney Kaiser
1st Place, Young Adult Division

Amongst the depthless sea becoming,
Amid my conscious thoughts and numbing.
My heart transcends its current state,
To join the faeries in its escape.
Mind reopened, doors unlocked,
Upon its ornate wood I knock.
To say hello to the great beyond,
A small ripple in this life pond.
A joint connection, a gear in place,
My words surpass this time and space.
An echo in this infinite realm,
But this isn't enough to overwhelm.
Craving more and reaching out,
A simple hello turns into a shout.
Knowledge unknown, forever unseen,
Ears are open, my eyes are keen.
A glimpse of starlight and nothing more,
And all these wonderments adore.
This perfect splendor and endless delight,
I see the stars that dance in the night.
Beauty so pure, all sin lives absent,
Impurities in these shattered fragments.
Glory beheld, light shone within,
A wonderful life, ready to begin.

I'm So Sad
Tracy Klinesteker
Senior Division

I'm so sad
We are broken
Beyond repair I think

Love doesn't seem
To work anymore
I don't know why

We are making plans
To leave
Talking quietly

Quitting, giving up
Throwing in the towel
Maybe it's for the best

I'm so sad
He is broken
There is nothing left to do

Nothing helps
Even silence hurts
No laughter anymore

I'm left with empty hands
And empty heart
Hanging by fingernails

I have to save myself
Or I will shrivel up
And blow away

I'm so sad
It's done

End of the Crucible
Ross Landers
1st Place, Adult Division

Dirt.
Hills.
Rocks.
The sun sets.
Orange sky.
Boots pound the ground.
I have my pack.
Inside is extra skivvies, spikes, a shelter half, gas mask, MREs.
My sleeping bag is strapped to the top.
I have my flak jacket.
I have my load bearing vest.
The pouches contain empty magazines.
I have my war belt.
It has empty grenade pouches.
And my two canteens.
My rifle is slung over my right shoulder.
My helmet sits on my head.
Its strap is snug around my chin.
A platoon of 80.
Broken up into two lines.
Both sides of the path.
Drill Instructors patrol up and down the middle.
Smokey hats.

Some recruits have fallen.
Some have dropped their gear.
Some are being smoked.
Up and down the line they run.
In full gear.
Sweat.
Heavy breathing.
Hungry.
Thirsty.
Sleepy.
The guide's flag flutters further down the line.
Platoon 3035.
Indigo.
The boots are heavy.
There will be bloody blisters to tend to.
Dirt crunches between my teeth.

America's True Horror Story
Hanna Laughery
2nd Place, Young Adult Division

You don't acknowledge me, don't like to think about me
Assuming you don't witness me every day that I'm not your problem
Dreaming of other nations overseas and believing "this problem couldn't be here"
Except you don't understand, I'm not who you want me to be
I'm your neighbor, your friend, your spouse, your child
And no matter what you want to think, I am all around you
A disease that's plaguing the land, except you created me
I'm your worst nightmare, America's true horror story
You have denied my existence within your borders, yet all I think about is your existence
And all the misery that they have performed on me because of you
They've beaten me and destroyed all the friends I have ever made
I've watched others disappear until all that was left was a body for them to use
You think viruses are the kings of depersonalization, well I know the Queen
And everything bows to it until I and all I know is forgotten
Expect that is when you want us, when they sell us to you
Broken and beaten, but you don't care as they slit our throats and feed you lies
I'm your worst nightmare, America's true horror story
You don't want me, I don't fancy me either
I stroll alone on streets crowded and filled with loud noises
Perceiving a world free to move as they please, while I am locked in chains so tight
I don't blame you, how could you possibly understand the horrors I've gone through
And I'm only the age of eleven
I've only looked at a distance of others my age
Playing with their beaming faces and learning with more books than I could ever imagine
But I know that will never be me
I've seen where I will end up and the grave seems like a better place than this cruel, cruel world
The sad thing is, you'll never locate me and I'll never escape

I'm not a missing person, I was sold into this and death is the only escape from this nightmare
I know that murder, suicide, or disease shall claim my body and I've expected my fate
I'm your worst nightmare, America's true horror story
You have forgotten about me over and over and over again
I've done so much for you, given all that I have and yet you only do little
You thought you freed me with your proclamation
Slavery has existed for generations before America and it'll exist long after
But my value has decreased to you
They say humans are priceless, yet my value is less than a hundred dollars
So maybe I deserve this if my worth is so low
I must have done something to deserve all this pain and suffering that they force onto me
Over and over again, I must satisfy them or they'll beat me and hurt me, but they won't kill me yet
I'm your worst nightmare, America's true horror story
I don't think you understand, otherwise, you might stand up and fight for my life
Fight for my freedom and justice as you have for so many others
You have allowed them to continue thriving off of me so I will die alone
My lifeblood on your hands, drenching you in scarlet and ruining the world
If you were to paint my brothers and sister in red, the world would be bathed in our blood
I eat and breathe the same air as you and yet you continue to ignore me
Thus I have become lost in who you think I am and who I know I am
I am everywhere you look and yet you have ignored me
And scorned me away so I have become trapped, unable to leave the lie you force on me
I'm your worst nightmare, America's true horror story
I'm your worst nightmare, America's true horror story
A victim of modern-day slavery, trapped in human trafficking
My life has become chains without keys
Locked in my head, locked in my heart, locked to the wall
Please help me
Please save me before it is too late
For I fear, I dread all that comes at me
I'm your worst nightmare, America's true horror story

Salute to our Soldiers
Mark Lego
Senior Division

A salute to our soldiers who protect this country
Through all your courage we are able to be free

Our troops are so valiant as they're ready to fight
And will secure our nation by our GOD given rights

For we can never imagine what a soldier goes through
Yet know they'll be there for the red, white and blue

We will support our troops who live in harm's way
And give honor to them in our prayers every day

Our freedom is not free as it comes with great cost
We should always remember the brave ones we've lost

For our stars and stripes, we are so honored to stand
To respect our armed forces who preserve this great land

To all of our military, may GOD watch over you
And comfort the families as faith guides you through

The sacrifices you make would be the hardest part
Which shows the character that comes from your heart

As an eagle soars over our land of the free
Proud soldiers are here to defend our liberty

For those standing for freedom, in our world of unrest
We Thank You for serving. May you be truly blessed.

Hope
Stephanie Lewman
3rd Place, Adult Division

The Demon dwells inside
Making it impossible to hide
Whispering horrible, believable lies
Over and over until it becomes my disguise.

Fight the demon that lives within.
Stand up to the bastard to save your own skin.
Take back your life. Push back with your all.
Embrace your power. Remember who you are!

Diminish the demon's worth
As it was done to you.
Turn the tables and try something new.
Light the flames within and let it burn.
For darkness will never go away,
But the light will always return.

Asphodel
Jacob Miller
3rd Place, Young Adult Division

I approached a woman in the field,
Being bent over collecting the midday grain.
She was swathed in colorful robes and
Anointed with gems under the skin.
Her eyes,
Though plain,
Had nothing but beauty in them.
Her skin had seen a thousand moments
And the summer that belonged to it.
She took my hand and said,
"My child,
Why are you lost?"
After a moment I paused and asked,
"Why must we always search for the meaning?"
She simply nodded for me to continue.
"Grandmother,
What are dreams?"
"They are simply the memories of tomorrow."
"Grandmother,
I do not remember."
"And so it has been."

And then I woke up.

Trees had Souls
RJ Robertson-DeGraaff
Young Adult Division

When I was five I thought trees had souls. Dead people were buried in the ground and trees grew out of the ground. I knew the actors in movies looked up at the sky when they spoke about heaven. I'd never seen a bible.

I have seventeen first cousins on one side, going to good Christian schools, eight aunts and uncles, graduates of good Christian colleges. My Papa led a prayer at every holiday. Prayer meant massive circles of hand-holding or respectfully looking at the ground before you could eat.
My mothers left their churches; they spoke about God the way they spoke about men. Oppressive, mostly inconvenient. Only a man would be dumb enough to connect our kitchen light switch to the bathroom.

My sophomore year, I'd decided that white men and the Catholic Church were the worst things to happen to world history.

I have seen a ghost.
She turns on faucets and throws textbooks. Once, she stole my ballet shoe.
The kids have conversations with her shadow- she doesn't like loud music,
I don't know if she is supposed to cross over somewhere
or if like me, she wasn't sure.

I know the texts are wrong (religion was created as a means of controlling the poor masses)
people need there to be meaning, an afterlife
I know they're fools, their belief gives it power.
When I hit a deer going 55mph,
I asked to be saved
could feel the tightness across the back of my skull.

A prayer to Nobody.

Oh We Wish
Lillian Ross
1st Place, Junior Division

Human

The wind in my hair
The sea at my back
The beautiful birds singing overhead
Oh what joy it would be
To be in the sea like a mermaid
Swimming away
Tasting the salty ocean
Feeling the water in my hair
Jumping through the waves
Swimming with my dolphin friends
Hearing the whales' song
Oh, what fun it would be.

Mermaid

When I break through the surface
The wind smells as salty as the sea itself
So I wonder and wonder
What if I was a human?
Feeling the wind in my hair
Seeing the birds flying overhead
Hearing their beautiful song
Walking on the boardwalk
Tasting cold ice cream
Cartwheeling over the sand
Running with my friends
Oh, I wish I could be human.

Summary
Finnegan Ross
Junior Division

Sweet sprinklers on my trampoline

Underdogs on the swing

Marshmallows over the fire

Memories from Nanee Camp

Eating ice cream outside

Riding on my razor scooter

Scotland
Eleanor Ross
Junior Division

Over the highlands and lowlands

Under the white and blue

In the land of legends

There's always a place for you.

You might see Nessie

You might just see fish

You might see a thistle and eat a Haggis dish.

You might wear your family kilt,

And play the bagpipe too.

No matter what you like,

Scotland is the place for you.

Between
Ailia Shaak
Adult Division

How did it happen?
  Just like anything does,
    One second at a time.

Like

  So

    Many

      Leaves

        Off

          A

            Tree

Falling to the ground
  One after another
    Dancing after their predecessors.

The petals of a flower
  Slowly coming unfurled
    Opening up to the call of spring.

Awakening

  Unfolding

    Becoming

      Blooming

        Into

          Itself

            At last

How does anything happen?
  With a quick, resolved breath,
    And a determined hand.

    It
      All
        Blurs
          Together
        Into a
          Thick
            Fog

A rolling sea of thought
  Clouds of memories twisted together
    Mixed with twinkling dreams.

A swirling mist
  Obscuring the details, and the truth
    And becoming the truth.

I'm
  Caught
    In
      A
        Memory
          Between
            Memories

How long before I get lost here?
Will I look at the forest, and see
  It has already shaken itself bare.

Because
  Afterwards
    There
      Is
        No
          Turning
            Back

One moment, I am singing to the fresh earth.
With the blink of an eye, the fields bloom,
And in another, they wither.

Will I notice the still moments between?
The second each new petal breaks free?
Or will I only remember the flower?

It's
  Sad
    To
      Say
        I
          Won't
            Remember.

So then, how does it end?
Just as everything comes to an end,
In one irreversible instant.

What
  Once
    Was
      There
        Is simply
          No
            Longer

The wind whispers abandoned songs
Only the roots remember the sun
    Streams press tightly into shivering mirrors.

The earth forgets your name,
But the leaves grow back
And the flowers bloom again.

An awakening, the beginning.
Something and everything
suddenly from nothing.
Origins that shall never be deciphered,
Or fully agreed upon.
There is only the absolute
That everything is,
And has
Possibly always been.

Yet we look to the stars,
Press ourselves close to the earth
And we wonder.
As those before us have wondered.

Inventing stories and legends
To explain it all.
The everything,
that as far as we know
Can never be explained.

Still we press our hearts to the soil
Dig deep into webs of mystery,
Philosophy and fantasy.
As if the answer
Could ever truly satisfy our hunger.
So I like to think,
The passion that humanity craves
In reality
Lies only in the questions.

Who?
What?
How?
When?

So precious that we compose mighty ballads.
So integral to humanity
That we tear each other to pieces
For the sake of our legends.
Are we not then
Confused animals
Baying wildly in the night,
Weathering the storms
Created by ourselves?

But the wolf does not ask why
He howls into the darkness.
The wolf does not ask,
Why is the moon?
The rabbits in their Warren
Know only that they must
Without fail
Always outrun the wolf.
For that is what nature dictates to be true.

Invisible,
yet just as gravitational
The questions tug at humanity.
Wrenching us through the fray of life.
The dreamers, and madmen,
The prophets spinning tales
Of the beginning,
And of course
The end.

Always, since the beginning of everything
Has loomed in the distance
At the back of humanity's skull,
The end.
For everything, even in nature
Comes to an end.
This is the madman's reasoning
As he shouts his philosophy
Into the maelstrom of human consciousness.

The pauper poets,
Accomplished minstrels, and preachers.
Every fanatic, and gloomy lover,
Since the formation of speech
Has tried to surmise,
And predict, the end.
Fascinated with finality.
Resignation to the end,
Always the end.

For within the very first second of creation
However grand and optimistic,
Are we not already
Hurtling towards the end?
As something new begins
It has started its journey,
Taken its first step
Towards
An eventuality.

Why?
Why?
Why?
Why...

If all we know in absolute
Is that there was a beginning,
And there will be an end.
Stay then, in the moment
That the first flower opens.
Stay then, in the arms
Of someone dear to your heart.
Live now,
For the moments between.

Hold close those still mornings
Of lover's kisses, and
Soft raindrops into the ground.
Marvel each time
You notice a new bud
Blooming to life in the landscape.
Celebrate that you were here
After the beginning,
But before the end.

I'm caught in a memory
Between memories
How long before I get lost here?
The wind whispers abandoned songs
Only the roots remember the sun
Streams press tightly into shivering mirrors.
The earth forgets your name,
But the leaves grow back
And the flowers bloom again.

Broken Beauty
Mark Stucky
1st Place, Senior Division

Glamour is a hollow, shiny shell,
a rapid, pretty paint job
on an insubstantial surface,
that alluringly promises much
but never satisfies the hunger.

True human beauty is internal,
from the depths of one's core.
It starts in the heart and soul.
It slowly sprouts and spreads,
percolates and permeates
the exterior from within.

The best but bleakest beauty
grows from wisdom
wrestled and wrought
from woundedness.
Pain, a teacher of distinction,
comes to every one of us,
but only some students
embrace the lessons
and find meaning in affliction.

For perceptive learners,
crises cut and clear the clutter
from bloated, busy lives,
enabling the complex splendor
of sorrow and healing,
of tears and laughter,
of doubt and faith,
of truth and grace,
of peace and joy,
of love and compassion
to emerge from pruned spaces.

Hope
Christine Webb
2nd Place, Adult Division

It's the spark that lights up a night before flickering out

It's the whiff of cookies as you walk through a strange house

It's the first flower of spring bravely blooming through snow

It's that moment after being lost when you know where to go

It's a wave that hits the shore and wipes the sand clear

It's the tiny white spots on a small baby deer

It's being lonely then seeing the face of a friend

It's watching a river disappear 'round a bend

It's the house that made it through a hurricane

It's that complicated math problem finally explained

It's a dog that discovered a long-lost bone

It's the name of your love lighting up your phone

It's a baby's hand grasping your pinky

It's the frosting in the middle of a twinkie

It's a faultless, smooth stone that's perfect to skip

It's printing your boarding pass for a trip

It's the first rays of sun after a dark storm

It's the first sip of hot chocolate keeping you warm

When grief threatens to take you, and you don't know how to cope

You have to hold on to a small piece of hope

FICTION

The Escape
Ralph Ackley
1st Place, Senior Division

He looked at his soiled clothes, tattered and torn from days of running from the law, trying to stay ahead of the sheriff, his deputies and their pack of dogs. He was already overwhelmed with fatigue. Now, as he faced the raging stream before him, he wondered if he should give himself up and tell the truth, the truth about what really happened, how his girlfriend had turned away so quickly from him that she fell against the blunt edge of an old oak. The impact knocked her to the ground and she died instantly. He panicked and without thinking, ran from the scene. The volatile history of their relationship was such that it would be extremely difficult for anybody in law enforcement in their tiny town of Libby, Montana to believe that there had been no physical abuse in that last moment before her accidental death. He had already spent 15 days in the Lincoln County jail for a previous domestic abuse charge.

She had bailed him out then and refused to press charges. He remembered feeling extremely grateful and indebted to her. For a while, things were good between them. He felt he had a handle on his temper and they were getting along really well, but she seemed to know all the right buttons to push and his rage returned the next argument they had, down at the park near the now raging Kootenai River. However, this time, he caught himself and stopped just before launching out in a physical attack. She reacted from previous experience and backed away out of instinct. That's when she fell away, backward into the oak tree. The faint echo of blood hounds barking in the distance shook him from his reverie. There wasn't a whole lot of time to make a decision. Should he cross or not?

The swift stream water, fed from the pregnant waters of the Kootenai, gathered quickly around his midsection as he moved cautiously forward in a slight diagonal across the swollen stream beneath Snowshoe Peak. Early autumn rains had been especially heavy the last few days, drenching the once parched ground with increasing frequency and intensity as the week wore on. The raging storms descended upon the Cabinet Mountains of northwestern Montana in a violent fury of water, flooding all the major rivers and streams. A wet madness filled small thirsty canyons, once dry river beds and obscure places that had never being flooded. The park rangers had never seen it rain this much nor had they ever observed so much flooding in such a specific area. This small range of Rockies north of the more famous Bitterroot Mountains had recently experienced one of the states' worse droughts in history. Most of the area was familiar to the man in the ragged, soiled clothes, fighting desperately against the current of the stream. He had grown up on a horse ranch near the small town of Libby, but this particular region seemed strangely unfamiliar. It made the effort to outwit his pursuers all the more difficult, yet he knew couldn't stop. He had to keep moving.

Slowly, he maneuvered his body forward against the swollen waters pressing in upon him as he approached the deepest section of the stream. He wondered if the local authorities had been able to track him over the last two miles through the low sage brush leading to the bottom of a nearby ravine. Though the rains had stopped, the muddy conditions made it difficult to hide his footprints. Because of this, he looked for as many streams and rivers to cross as possible. He picked his way carefully across the pebbled bed with bare feet, feeling for every step. He resisted the natural tendency to lift his legs and walk against the current, knowing the added mass would easily suck him under. His limbs were getting colder. Numbness was beginning to settle in. The fresh rainwater was a much needed and welcomed godsend. Yet, because of the icy, September rains; it was hard to be thankful.

The numbness increased, coursing through his extremities. He worried that it wouldn't be long in these mountain-fed streams before he experienced the first effects of hypothermia. He had read that after only ten minutes, a person's muscles would begin to feel the early symptoms. In an hour, confusion, complete exhaustion and possibly death would result.

Don't panic! He though. Stay alert!

His Daddy's words echoed in his mind: "You can't beat nature. Respect her power. Give in where you can and work with her. She's not out to get you, son. Whatever you do, don't panic. Stay alert. Stay calm."

He dragged his water-logged legs to the left and then slightly right through the weight of the water. It was becoming increasingly difficult to make any progress. Glancing back over his shoulder, he looked at the current he already traversed and noticed he had slowed considerably. He wondered where the posse was and thought he heard the echo of the dogs again in one of the nearby canyons but he blew it off as just a product of his increasing anxiety.

He spied the apparent safety of a flat area of swollen stream tempting him to veer off course and move to the upper right but resisted. Instead, looking away to the left, he balanced himself to gain a better footing and plodded toward a parallel area of water that was much more active. This seemed like a highly unreasonable thing to do but somewhere deep in his gut, he felt an ancient instinct kick in. Though his muscles ached terribly, he continued, stopping briefly to glance at the skies overhead. It had been nearly seven minutes since he entered the flooded stream. Smaller ripples flowed in perfect symmetry across a section about six feet square, eventually slowing toward a flat, shallow shoreline that bordered a length of sand bar toward the northwest. Despite the icy temperature of the water, he moved ahead, propelled by the mysterious inner feeling that stirred inside of him. He had to stay calm. There was a considerable body of water yet to cross. Moving prodigiously onward, he became keenly aware of the need to find dry land as quickly as possible. He came to the middle of the stream and was surprised to find less depth. He was now only inches away from the ripple section that promised a shallower bottom.

As he exhaled, he deliberately slowed his breathing down and spoke to himself, repeating his words like a Hindu mantra: "Careful now. Easy does it. Careful now. Easy does it."

He approached the ripples and felt the shallower bottom with his feet, dragging them diagonally through the stream. The water level had dropped even further and the current had slowed up as well. He breathed a sigh of relief, stumbled toward the sand bar and collapsed from fatigue. He was completely spent, having exhausted his body from the emotional and physical strain of the crossing. A hawk circled above him as the sun began to peek out from behind a lingering thunderhead, pregnant from the past rain of the week, seeking to join the rest of the storm's clouds dissipating toward the south. He laid his head down against a fifteen-foot slice of weathered, white-bark pine that was struck years ago by a bolt of lightning. It had been carried downstream by another heavy autumn rain years ago, fetched up along the sandbar and dried out in the sun. The strong winds subsided and the skies cleared. A warm, afternoon sun came out. At first, he fought sleep, fearing the recurring nightmare of dogs and men chasing him with guns and bullhorns through the winding back roads, endless trails and rivers. Soon, his thoughts crashed in on themselves and exhaustion took over. He gave in and soon fell into a deep sleep.

Hours later, he awoke with a shiver. His first sight as he turned on his back was the Milky Way. The skies had cleared and the expanse of stars twinkling their warmth, millions of light years away from him brought him back to the memories of his childhood, camping outside of his house with his dad and little brother. His mind was a bit foggy but he soon remembered where he was and why. The stream raged on. It jogged his mind and he listened for what was sure to be the sheriff's department and their dogs hot on his heels again. Would he ever be able to hide his scent and loose them? He sat up and listened carefully. An owl hooted. The flutter of its wings as it swept down through a ridge of pine behind the sand bar spooked him. He could hear no barking or rustling of bodies in the nearby forest. Still, it wasn't safe for him to go back to sleep. They may be close by camped out in the forest. He figured it must be about 4 am. If he started walking now, he could make some headway and be that much further ahead of them. He had to try and find ways to hide his scent as he walked on. Stumbling as he got up, he found that his limbs still ached and the muscles in his calf were still cramped. It took a while for him to get his bearings. He stretched and looked down over the sand bar, beyond the swamp to the left. He could barely make out an old woods road, overgrown from years ago. He got up and headed toward the black forest, not really knowing where he was going, just trying to stay ahead.

The Life of a Priceless Pen
Grace Flanagan
2nd Place, Young Adult Division

It always bent to the will of its master, but what credit can you give it for that? It had no choice but to toil daily for the boy. And when not in use, it rested snug in its wooden case dreaming of stories it would inscribe on paper. It was given no name, pen was all it was called. It possessed no life other than that given to it by its master. It may have had no purpose other than to serve its master, but it lived its purpose to the full.

The pen's master was sad, for unlike his pen, the boy didn't know his purpose. He wrote with a certain mindlessness stemming from unfulfilled dreams. He merely employed the pen daily to forget everything else in his life. It was in this way the pen came to know the boy, for it gave voice to his silent heart.

The pen always loved to think of the first thing it ever wrote: "love." The words that followed it were less beautiful, but no less important for they spoke truly of the emotions of the writer. It was the pen that wrote them by the hand of the writer, and then pen grimaced to know such ugly words, yet he later learned that even the ugly thoughts and writings were of purpose, for once they are acknowledged they can be removed. This is what the pen helped the boy acknowledge, "Love," the boy had scratched on paper, "is of no consequence. It has never given me anything worthwhile in life, neither happiness nor sorrow." The pen did not like to write this. It knew that love was useless if all you hoped was to gain by it, but it also knew that love is wonderful if you seek to lose for it, because that is what love is, losing part of yourself for someone else. How could the pen tell the boy this? It only had life as the boy gave to it, ideas it could process only as they were introduced to it. It could create nothing on its own. When the pen saw that the boy was throwing away love at his young age for want of gain and could not speak to warn the boy of his misconceptions, it could only employ two of the greatest weapons for healing a wounded soul, patience and time.

Four years passed as the pages of the old leather-bound journal began the first stages of breaking down and the pen sat silent in its snug silky case.

When daylight entered the case, the pen leapt for joy, for its master had returned to it, but like his journal the boy had begun to break down, he now wrote worse things of his life. The pen wrote not of cynical world views now, but of pure and unadulterated sorrow. A heart shattered into silence. Its beat forever lost amid the sound of tears splattering the pages and the furious scratch of the pen on the paper. The pen learned that cynicism was gone from the boy's heart for good, and he was a man now. He was one who lost his heart for want of a return of love, but as the pen drew up the pages of man's dampered thoughts it was glad that the man had learned just how consequential love was.

Ten more years faded into time, and the pen wondered if the man had gone forever. Finally, the day creeped into the creaking case, and the pen felt the warmth of the man's fingers on its cold metal, fingers burning with a white hot rage, and the pen feared the thoughts it would write. But the pen wrote nothing this time, for it was thrown hard into a wall of the man's bedroom. Time stood still as the pieces drifted to the ground with its own breaking heart, its master had loved it to life, now it was being thrown into death. The pen sat shattered for, how many days? It felt like years to the dying pen, with no thoughts to write, only suffering to withstand.

An eternity later, when the velvet hand of a woman picked the pen up and placed it back whole into its soft case, the pen wondered for the absence of the man. Suddenly it was being picked up, thrown in a bag, and hurried into a trunk packed to the brim. The suffocating hours of being saved from death, yet wondering where its master was were a toil on the pen's patience. It wondered what its master had learned, if anything at all. Then it was being taken out of the suitcase, thrown into another bag and carried bumpily for several hours. When it was removed from the bag and from its case it was placed in the soft grasses of foreign lands. Its master had returned. The pen waited eagerly for the man to write. When he did it was with softness and tenderness. He spoke of all his life. Books he read, dreams he'd dreamed, tears he'd shed, and laughs he'd laughed. Then he said now he was content. He understood that he didn't know anything about life, and that he didn't need to, he needed only to experience it. Live through it. He said he lived his life neglected and broken by everyone around him, but now he no longer placed any faith in others. He said his only value was that his Master gave him. His life too was only given to him by his Master, and therefore he could be patient, all things would come to him in time.

And that was the last of the man's precious thoughts of the heart the pen ever recorded. It wrote many times of other events of the man's life, but never again of his heart.

One day the ink dried up and the pen was placed in a grave the man had made for it among nature. Then the man bent down and spoke to the pen. He said, "All your life you never sought anything but to serve me with patience. You never taught me with anything but silence, and you never lived any life but the one you received from my hand. Now you have nothing more to give me, but you have already given me everything I need." He breathed deeply, "You gave me knowledge of my own heart, understanding of my own thoughts, love for my own life, and that is enough."

Crouching Tiger
Mark Giacabone
3rd Place, Senior Division

Every evening our nine-pound tuxedo tom cat seemingly transforms into a 210-pound puma with saber teeth and an attitude for the outdoors. He stands by the back door holding a demanding stare.

We open the door and quickly release him to avoid losing furniture and limbs.

With the first paw on grass he transforms the Schoolcraft Prairie into the South Serengeti.

Everything gets quiet… from crickets to coyotes.

After a night of hunting and occasional "Fight Club" (he never talks about it) he returns to the kitchen window to reclaim his domain.

His breakfast includes 15 pounds of raw meat (4 oz. of Meow Mix). He then forces his way to the TV room, turns on the National Geographic channel and spends the day snoozing on the sofa (Couching Tiger).

We don't ask any questions and we don't interfere but we hid the car keys and locked up the liquor.

Advice: If your pet wants something… and their eyes go red…

just give it to them.

The "Treat"
Katie Grossman
2nd Place, Adult Division

I woke up to the smell of chocolate chip cookies wafting through the house. My mom's cookies were the absolute best cookies in the world. Jumping out of bed as quickly as possible, I ran down the hall to find out why she was making cookies this morning.

"Mom, can I have one? What are they for?" I peppered her with questions.

"Well, I thought it would be nice for you to take a treat into school today. You can wait to have yours with your classmates," she replied.

What a great idea, I thought. I watched as she carefully loaded the warm cookies into the Tupperware container and sealed it tightly with care. Racing back to my room, I wanted to quickly get dressed. Knowing it was going to be a wonderful day, I selected my royal-blue corduroy jumper and my matching patchwork royal-blue and yellow shirt. The rest of the morning flew by as I waited in anticipation of pulling up to school with my treat. I already loved school, and this would just make it even better!

I have always been a very quiet kid, some would say painfully shy, but today was going to be a gamechanger, I just knew it. When my mom dropped me off in the ramp, I proudly carried my treats into my classroom. Marching right up to my teacher, Mrs. Bell, I proclaimed,

"I brought a treat!"

Mrs. Bell replied, "Oh, that is wonderful. I didn't realize it was your birthday today. We will have it after lunch!"

In that moment, I froze and couldn't say anything. I immediately put my head down and proceeded to my desk, quickly pulling out my pencils. The teacher loudly announced to the class,

"We will be having a special treat later to celebrate Katie's birthday!"

My cheeks burned and my heart started pounding. I could not look at any of my classmates in that moment. It was not my birthday. But, the train was already down the tracks and there was nothing I could do to stop it at that point. The pit of my stomach felt like it had a rock in it. For the rest of the morning, my concentration was completely lacking. The day dragged on, and I couldn't even muster the enthusiasm when meeting the letter person of the day, Mr. M. Usually, I would get such joy out of the letter people, but not today.

Just after lunch, Mrs. Bell presented me with a purple construction paper crown covered in glitter. She placed it on my head and called me to the front of the classroom to perch on the birthday stool. The whole class then sang "Happy Birthday" to me, while I stared at the floor wishing I could sink into it. Everyone loved the cookies, but I couldn't even really enjoy mine. My mouth was too dry and I felt slightly sick. The end of the day bell finally rang and I trudged out into the hallway with my bedazzled crown, my empty Tupperware container and my wounded pride. Looking up, I saw my mom staring at me with a curious expression on her face. Then, to my dismay, she walked right over to Mrs. Bell and told her it wasn't my birthday! As if I wasn't already mortified enough, she had to spell it out to her. Oh, the embarrassment I felt. I am actually surprised I passed kindergarten after that fiasco. And my mom never sent a treat again…except on my actual birthday!

She Gave it a Try
Marilyn Jones
2nd Place, Senior Division

It was a sad day for Betsy
Already she was pushing forty-seven,
Her hubby died young with cancer
She has forty more years
Before thinking of Heaven.

Her three children are grown
They all moved away,
She tried volunteering, it was okay
But how will she spend every lonely day?

She was invited to a barbecue
And met a guy there,
He was well dressed (and single)
With a little gray in his hair.

He liked her looks
And asked her out on a date,
This could get interesting
Perhaps it was fate.

Her neighbors were nosy
She always seemed to be on the phone,
If she had a gentleman friend
It's nobody's business but her own.

She giggled a lot
He thought she had lots of money,
That's when he made his move
And called her, "My sweet Bit-O-Honey."

She had started on the "Pill" again
As she didn't want any little surprise,
As for kinky positions, she faked it
With a little compromise.

She had purchased some lacy undies
So was prepared… just in case,
After eating out one evening
They ended up back at her place.

The lights were dimmed
Sinatra was crooning, "I did it my way",
He fumbled with her hook and eye
Her stretch marks were showing
But she relaxed with a sigh.

Good Lord, what was he thinking?
He should know I don't bend that way,
And her sinuses dripped on every kiss
They decided to do it better another day.

He took her dining and dancing one night
She splurged – had two glasses of wine,
He was pretty good at the two-step
She got woozy, was ready for bed by nine.

Her kids had lots of questions
What do you know about this guy?
The even had an intervention
It made her cry.

He wondered where the life insurance went
After assuming she lived on "Easy Street",
He caught her juggling bills one day
And realized she could barely make ends meet.

Betsy now knew that bodies mature
There was nothing wrong with her,
She did forget to pluck a whisker on her chin
But looked darned good, for the shape she's in.

She decided to let him down gently
Told him she didn't want to see him anymore,
He was relieved and called here a whore,
As he left her house, he slammed the door.

Affairs don't always end well
All she wanted was a little affection,
It was obvious he had a sweet tooth
And wanted the entire confection.

Scarlett O'Hara was spunky and strong
She shook her fist at God, to pray,
Rhett Butler said "He didn't give a damn"
While she muttered, "Fiddle-dee-dee,
Tomorrow is another day."

As Fate Would Have It
Hannah Laughery
3rd Place, Young Adult

"We have to go." Callie, my twin sister whispered to me, crying. I could feel my body shaking all over the place. What did she want? And why did we have to leave? I grabbed my big glasses and slid them on, moving my short dark brown hair out of my face.

The glasses didn't do much to help. It was pitch black, nighttime. I turned to my left as I sat up. It was only 3:45 in the morning. Why was I awake? Better yet, why was Callie?

"Stella." I watched her shadow move away from my bed as she spoke. "I did something." She grabbed what looked like a bag off of the floor. "Something really bad and we have to go, I know we just settled into our foster family. But…" She started shoving items into the bag. "I'm scared and we… and…it doesn't matter, we have to go."

"What about Mark, isn't he your boyfriend?" I asked her as I stood up, my blanket hitting the floor.

"Not anymore." She said. Her voice strained as she stopped moving and just dropped like a weight on the floor, tears leaking from her eyes like a waterfall. I quickly ran to her. She was my lifeline, the strong one. She was strong as we moved from foster home to foster home, and even before when our mother used to abuse us and almost killed us. Callie was my rock and now she was crumbling.

What did he do to her?

I grabbed her from the floor and she sobbed in my embrace. "I'll help Callie. I'll get us away, he won't be able to hurt you again." I whispered into her ear as I ran my hand through her dark brown curls. "Get changed and cleaned up, I'll finish packing for us." She nodded her head as she leaned back wiping her tears.

I grabbed the bag from her as she went to the bathroom right outside our bedroom. The light was always on in the hallway so I could just see her painted nails as she left.

We never kept secrets from each other. We only had two rules - to never leave each other, and to always be honest to each other. We had been through too much already for it to be any different. Not all of the foster homes we had been to had been nice, so we had always had a to-go bag on hand. Always knew how to pack in a hurry. In the span of minutes.

"Ready?" Callie said as she entered the room. I nodded my head and put on the backpack. I made sure we each had two changes of clothes, 200 dollars, and some hygiene products. I had already called a taxi and pulled out the money for one to get us to the bus station.

"Yes."

She grabbed my hand, leading me through the window and onto the tree. I tried not to look down. I wasn't very good with heights and balancing. I started to feel my foot slip and looked up at Callie, fear stark in my eyes.

"Help!" I whispered, trying not to freak out.

She helped me regain my balance and soon we were out of the high tree and onto the safe ground. I wanted to kiss the ground. I was so happy to be on it, but I knew we needed to leave.

"I called a taxi while you were in the bathroom, it's close." Making sure we were still holding each other's hand, so to not lose each other, we ran to the taxi. We were both active so we made it in no time.

I opened the door to the taxi, ushering in Callie. "To the bus station please." I told him like Callie had so many times before. Now it was my turn to be brave.

"You the lady that called?"

"Yep."

The bus station was huge. And even being so early in the morning, the place was alight with sounds and color. Signs with places all over America showed on several boards and I could see all the buses waiting to depart. This was the sixth bus station that we had been to together in our lives. By now the foster care system knew our tactics so they would know to look here first, but this time we weren't going back to the foster care system. I could tell that this time was different. Whatever we were running from would be waiting for us if we ever got caught. It was time to leave Chicago. We walked over to the line for tickets. The line wasn't terribly long and soon we were at the counter. "Can we get two tickets to Detroit please?" Detroit was in Michigan, not too far away but there were many stops where we could get off, plus the tickets were only thirty dollars. The women pressed some buttons as I slid across the money.

The lady handed us the tickets. The bus left in ten minutes. We would arrive in Detroit at approximately 12:59. They allowed us to board early and as soon as we sat down, Callie curled up next to me, her head using my arm as a pillow. With my other arm, I pulled out a blanket for her. It was 68 degrees outside but I knew she slept better with one.

"Callie." I gently stabbed my finger into her side. She rolled over. "Callie, wake up."

"It's not time for school yet." She grumbled at me. I sighed, this was not the time for her to be sleepy.

"Callie, we're on the bus, remember." She sat up so fast I thought she would hit the window behind her. Her startled face scanned the bus before looking me up and down. It was the first sign of old Callie that I had not seen since yesterday, the Callie who was clear headed and not afraid, that is until she slowly sunk down and started to cry.

I held her in my arms and tried to shake her gently as the bus drove over the uneven road. "Stella, he hurt me. Over and over again. I barely escaped." She leaned away from my arms. I hadn't noticed until now that she was wearing long sleeves and jeans in spring. Usually she wore dresses and tank tops. Not this.

"Callie." I held out my hand and she gently put her arm in it. I lifted her sleeve so no one else in the bus could see. Deep purple and bright green marked her arms like a tapestry. "When did he do this?" She grabbed her hand from mine and shrunk into the corner. "He's been, but it wasn't bad. Not noticeable and he was so kind and then he would get upset and then be so sweet after that I... I.... and then last night, he wouldn't stop and..."

I leaned in closer to her, but she flinched away. "He hurt me Stella." She looked up at me. Through her tear stained lashes there was something I had never seen before…fear.

"Okay, I'm going to hand you the bag. We'll get off at this stop here. Don't let go of my hand." I heard her stomach growl loudly like a lion. "We'll get something to eat first. They shouldn't find us here."

We exited the bus in a city called Kalamazoo. It's between Detroit and Chicago, at least, that's what the map on the bus said. We walked along the sidewalk until we found a place for food, a small diner. Callie's eyes shifted everywhere, taking in our surroundings and people moving. I knew she was scared someone was going to hurt her like Mark had. But throughout our short life, I had learned that some people you could trust, like Callie, and some people you couldn't. Our mother and now Mark were on that list.

We entered the diner with a little bit of hesitation. We were hungry, but we didn't want to get in trouble. The sign in the front said to sit anywhere, so I dragged Callie with me to a booth in the back. We were out of the way and hopefully out of danger.

We waited.

After about ten minutes and Callie falling asleep again, I managed to wake her up and figured I should go ask for menus and water. They probably hadn't seen us come in. I didn't want to draw attention to us.

"Callie, I'm going to the bar. You think you'll be okay?"

"Yeah, you sure they won't find us?"

"Positive. We're not going back in the system and Mark won't find you ever." I stared into her eyes as I proclaimed my word. "I need you to stay awake, okay?"

"Yep." Looking her over one last time, I left for the bar.

"Is that your sister?" A woman next me leaned down and asked, pointing at the booth where Callie was watching me intently. Figuring it couldn't hurt, I nodded. "She's pretty and so are you, and so young to not be in school." The lady exclaimed. I started to freak, but having been through this before, calmed myself.

"No Ma'am, we may look young but I can assure you we're not in high school anymore."

"Oh, I see, running away?" I opened my mouth to refute but she kept talking. "I remember when I was 16, I ran away from my second foster home. You see, my first one had been so nice, but then they'd had a baby and they'd already adopted so many, so I was forced to leave. At my second place, the man would hurt me. So, I left. Haven't looked back since."

"Where did you go?"

"Many places." She got a faraway look in her eyes before focusing on me again. "But when I turned 17, I found this place called Sclábhaí. They take care of you and love you so you're never alone. They helped me become a working, earning member of society. It was what I needed to help me become the person I am today."

I looked up at her in admiration. Here was someone who had been in my shoes before, knew what it was like to run away and have to be strong. And she said that this place, this Sclábhaí helped her? Maybe they could help us too.

"Where are you from?" She asked.

"Many places." I answered as anonymously as she had. She laughed at my response and raised her glass of orange juice.

"Well then, here's to many places." I smiled at her proclamation. We both had been to many places, probably both would be to many more places. It was a really fitting toast.

A server finally came over to me and the lady. "What would you like?" He said blindly, looking only at his pad of paper and pen.

"Two orders of your French toast." I answered. We were short on money, but I could get a job somewhere, make more money. Maybe Sclábhaí was hiring?

"That all?" He asked, still not looking at me. "Yes please." I answered him politely. It was how my father had raised me, to be polite to others and have respect, even when it isn't given back. Figuring that was my cue to leave and go to Callie, I turned around and started heading towards the booth. I was halfway there when I felt an arm grab me. I nearly jumped ten feet in the air as I turned around to face whoever had found us.

"Relax, it's just me. I wanted to say I'm glad we talked. Us foster girls gotta stick together." She turned around and started to leave. I just stood there, tugging on my hair. I wanted to ask about Sclábhaí.

"Wait." I called out before she left the store.

"Yes?"

"Um... Since we're new here and all I... and you mention sticking together... Well, just, do you think Sclábhaí is hiring?" Her face visibly brightened. "They're always hiring. Why don't I interview you over breakfast and see if you're fit for Sclábhaí? By the way, I'm Sara." I nodded my head and led her over to Callie and our booth.

"Stella, who is this?" Sara and I sat down as I explained who Sara was and about Sclábhaí where we could work. Sara explained all that they did and how they helped make the community a better place to be and thrive, that age didn't matter. We could get a job there easily.

At the end of breakfast, Sara stood up and gave us her card. "The address is on there and you can show up on Monday at nine. Tell them I sent you and you should be all good." She beamed. "I'll see you then." She left, after paying for our meal.

I held her business card in my hand.

"Are you sure about this?" Callie asked as she finished her toast.

"Yes, we need this. We need a job if we're aren't going back and this place sounds so good."

"Almost too good to be true."

"Callie please, we need to work somewhere and this is a good opportunity." She sighed and ran her fingers through her hair.

On Monday, we walked into Sclábhaí.

"Hello, Sara sent us." I told the lady at the front desk. The place looked so friendly, little couches and tables lined the entrance. I knew it was right for us to go here.

"Right this way ladies." We followed the desk lady from the main room back into the compound. That's when the fear hit me. I turned around to try and escape, but two men had come up behind us and stopped me and Callie from leaving.

I woke up in complete darkness. We had been at Sclábhaí for months now, trained for a week before I was forced to have sex with complete strangers over and over again for money. Only 70 dollars per person. I wasn't worth much. None of us were.

I climbed onto the roof of the compound and walked along the edge. Just one wrong step and I would fall a couple hundred stories down. I was in Detroit, on top of one of their prestigious hotels where I worked sometimes. I had been trafficked from Kalamazoo to Detroit to Chicago following that path over and over. Every week, a different city. But I was in Kalamazoo most of the time. In some of the surrounding areas too.

I probably could have left by now, but they told me they'd kill Callie if I did. On the second day, we woke up together, bound and tied. They kept us together for training but after that I haven't seen her since.

I jumped off the edge and back onto the roof in my heels. There is no escape. I belonged to Sclábhaí.

Just a Moment
Sky Lester
1st Place, Young Adult

I know what I want. I've known what I wanted for a long time, but it's not something that I can just work towards and expect to receive. No, what I want is a moment. A moment in time that can't be repeated. A moment in time that can't be replicated or replaced. Everyone around me is getting what they want, but me, it just never works out. Is there something wrong with me? Are they better? Did they do something different? The bus jars my body and my mind as I latch onto the bar in front of me. If I didn't have the reflexes of a hawk, I would definitely be face first on the ground right now. Usually, a simple breath will clear my head of these doubts and fears, but today, it seems I need a little bit more.

With each stop we make, the bus gets a little more crowded, but it finally reaches the stop that I'm looking for. Carefully avoiding touching the other people, I snake my way to the front, exiting to the only place I want to be on days like today. At least I can take a breath here.

The park is as bright and beautiful as it always is, the afternoon sun landing perfectly on every tree and flower in sight. It draws more than just me in, the crowds clustered yet scattered. It's the only park in this part of the city, so anyone who has free time during the summer months usually comes here to spend their time. Today it's even busier than normal, but before I trek my way to my favorite spot, there is one stop that I have to make. "Dayton, would be pretty upset if he saw me walking around without one of his signature flowers." I head towards the center of the park, a semblance of a smile on my face.

The very center of the park is a stone circle with a patch full of flowers in the middle. The unofficial vendors that sell their wares have their tables set up at different points around the circles. Technically, they aren't supposed to sell here without a license, but no park attendant has ever stopped them.

Dayton's table is easy to spot since he always takes the spot closest to the drinking fountain, his table full of colorful hairpins in the shape of flowers. He's the only table I actually visit here since all the other vendors are just here to make a quick buck. The second that he spots me, his brown eyes light up. "My favorite customer! I'm glad to see the nice weather brought you back." Is there ever a day when he isn't happy? My response is a smile, his mood a good contender against my foul one. Some people are just inherently happy, and it isn't my place to put him in a bad mood because of my personal problems.

I look over the small batch he's brought in today, an array of colors and flowers before me. "Hmmm. It's always so hard to decide. Which one do you think goes best with my outfit?" We go through the same routine every time I come here, but it's always fun to talk to him. I pose with my arm on my hip, a genuine smile spreading on my face. It only takes a moment of looking for him to decide which one is best as he snatches a pink rose hairpin from his table.

Walking around the table, he personally puts it in my hair, smiling at his work on display. "This one hits all three. The pink matches the color of your dress, it brings a pop of color to your brown hair, and it highlights those sea-like teal eyes of yours." Ironic that the man who sells the most beautiful hairpins chooses to keep his own head bald. He is one of the few people who can pull it off and still look good, his copper skin shining in the sun. He returns behind his table, grabbing a mirror to show me his work. It looks pretty in my hair, and even though everything he said is true, I don't stare for very long. The sight and thought of myself is something I don't like to handle most days, and today, I can barely handle it for a second.

Regardless of the swirling thoughts starting in my head, I still smile, reaching into my purse and pulling out ten dollars. "I don't think I could've picked a better one. Thanks for always helping, Dayton." His eyes go wide at the sight of the money, his hand pushing it away for a moment. Another interaction we go through every time because he only charges a certain amount, and I always end up giving him more.

He shakes his head, showing his defiance for a moment. "You know that I only charge a couple of dollars for these things. Ten dollars is far too much for a simple hair pin, especially when I'm selling to someone as hard-working as you." I can't help but laugh, refusing to put my hand down. I only work hard at the job I have because I don't really have anything else to work towards right now.

With amusement in my voice, I explain, "This is for more than just the hairpins." He cocks his head like a confused puppy, but I set down the money and walk away before he can respond. The hairpins, more so the interaction, means far more to me than he realizes. That's why I always tend to give him more than the cost of one hairpin. I wave, calling back, "Thanks for the beautiful accessory. I'll be back soon." When he shakes his head, it just makes me laugh more, my retreat executed perfectly. He hasn't chased me down yet to return the money, so until the day that he does, I'll keep paying as much money as I want for them.

At first, the crowds surround me, but I quickly make my way towards a less populated path in the park. This path starts as pavement, but eventually leads to a dirt path, turning off most people who are here for the ease of walking rather than viewing the nature around them. That's what makes it so appealing to me on days like this. When my thoughts are my only company, I don't really like to be around other people.

My eyes track the people initially, happy couples holding hands, kids running around their parents, and small groups having picnics. They look so happy. When tears start forming in my eyes, I shift my glance towards the trees, the sun peeking through the leaves. Nature might not be enough to take my mind off things. I've spent so much time looking at these trees that I feel like I should be able to name each and every one, but since I've never studied trees, I just admire them as I walk by. The path is also lined with different kinds of flowers depending on where you walk. This one happens to have pink tulips. I'm sure that there are much more than that on other trails, but since I spend most of my time on this one path, I haven't explored many of the more populated trails to find out.

With each step I take towards the dirt path, the crowd gets thinner but so does my patience. The whole reason I came out here was to take my mind off of things, but the quieter that it gets, the louder my mind yells. Just focus on the breeze, the trees, and the flowers. A sigh escapes my lips, the flowers not a good enough distraction today.

The thoughts don't stop, like a swirling hurricane in my mind, until I make it to my favorite spot in the park. There is a small creek on the dirt path. The only way to cross it is a beautiful arched bridge made from red oak wood. When the sun hits it just right, it looks like something out of a fairy tale. I take a deep breath as I step up to the center of the bridge, looking out to the water underneath. No people around to show me what I'm missing. No people around to show me what I don't have. No people around.

It's people being around me that started this spiral in the first place. Everyone else around me is succeeding. It creates a rift between me and other people like we're all running a marathon, but I've had my ankles taken out by a baseball bat. My whole life I thought that hard work would lead to fulfillment, but the thing that I want isn't something I can't work towards. Love isn't a job that you can apply for. Skills don't matter, and most days it seems like the more you look for it, the less likely you are to find it. Love strikes hard and fast, a moment of lightning shared between two people. And the way my life has been going, it seems like a distant dream.

The tears start to fall as I stare at the river, looking into the water but not seeing anything.

This sight is beautiful, the clear, blue sky reflecting into the equally clear water, but this isn't what I want. All I want is somebody to share it with. The sound of a throat clearing hits me like a slap to the face, but I grip the side of the bridge to keep from jumping out of my own skin. There are usually so few people on this part of the trail that I didn't expect anyone to be here today. When I don't turn to face them, wiping the tears from my eyes, they walk up to the edge of the bridge, leaving some space between us.

"It's not often I find somebody else here. This spot is always beautiful at this time." His voice is soft but apparent in this space void of other people. I nod my head to agree, too embarrassed to say anything. He approaches again, "I like your hair pin, by the way. I've never seen one that matches the color of the flowers around here so perfectly." I can't help but laugh, disbelief and shock melding within me like lightning with no rain. Well if this is what comes of my moping then I might as well embrace it.

With no sobs or tears left, I state, "Thank you. I actually got it here in the park." I decide to finally face him, my eyes still shiny from crying, but they shine even brighter when I spot him. He is tall, his hair a chestnut brown, but that isn't what catches my attention. His eyes, bright green like the grass in spring, are staring right into mine, a small, but powerful, smile on his face. It's such a contrast to my foul mood that I can't help but smile myself, my cheeks turning red when I realize how long I've been staring. "My name is Nora, by the way." My eyes dart back to the water, overwhelmed by the presence of him.

He laughs, taking a step closer. "My name is Logan. So what brings you to my favorite part of the park?" I grab the edge of my dress tightly, nerves sparking off like a fire trying to start. Is it worth telling the truth?

While scratching my head, I explain, "I actually come here to clear my head. It's been a long day, and this place usually calms me down." It's better to tell him the truth and have him walk away than put up a front that would mislead him.

He nods his head like a piece of a puzzle is clicking into place. "Well this is a good place to do that. The water is a surprisingly good listener. Did you want to talk to the water alone?" I try to hide my laugh, but it comes out anyway. There is no way that I'd be able to speak my problems out loud. Besides, he might have been here first.

I shake my head, waving the suggestion off. "Since this is your favorite spot, I can find a different place to clear my head. The river probably doesn't want to listen today anyway." My heart aches as I turn away from him, but it's probably the right decision. He already helped a bit by making me smile, so the least I can do is let him enjoy his day.

I barely make it a step off the bridge before he calls out to me. "You know, I hear there is a willow on the other side of the park that is an even better listener. It listens to people's problems all day. Since we're both here, we could go check and see if it's true." Disbelief hits me first like a shock through my gut, but it eventually melts into relief. I don't realize that I am holding my breath until it comes flooding out of me. Does he actually want to spend more time with me?

With a smile, I turn back to him, finding him a few steps behind me. His smile is soft but his eyes are bright as if this answer will make or break him. It catches me off guard, but I respond, "An even better listener than the river? Seems like that does need investigating. I'd be happy to join if you'd have me." I watch the light dance in his eyes as he steps in next to me. His warmth is the first thing I notice, a shocking but happy surprise.

He seems even taller standing next to me, his height enough to block the sun from my eyes as we make our way across the park. This isn't exactly what I expected but not something I want to walk away from either. I keep glancing at him just to make sure he's real, finally getting caught in the process. "Something I can help with?" My cheeks blaze red under his eyes as I start to mess with my fingers. There is such a genuine kindness in his tone that I find myself smiling every time he talks.

With a timid tone, I admit, "You've already helped. I'm just happy to be here." Now his cheeks flare red, a smile spreading across my face at the sight. I can't believe that only a few moments ago I was panicked about so many things. It actually seems kind of stupid now with somebody so bright standing next to me. I know what I want. All I want is a moment that will change everything, but that's the funny thing about moments, you don't know their value until they end.

Valley Forge
By Hayden Moden
1st Place, Junior Division

12-10-1777

Dearest Margaret,

My life here in Valley Forge is much more unyielding than I expected. We have mere cloths to wrap our feet in the bone chilling cold of the winter. I've gotten frostbite more times than I can count. I miss the roasted goose and corn you made, it is heaven compared to the horrendous hard lump they give us, whom they call "firecake." I do not care what it is called, it tastes like sand and never makes me full. So, I am left sitting here by a fire, my feet black from frostbite, wrapped in a flimsy piece of cloth to keep me warm, and ravenous for a home cooked meal.

That buffoon, Washington, has been talking about an attack and how we can do this, but I believe it is just a bunch of hogwash. I mean no disrespect to our general, but we have been losing fight after fight, soldier after soldier, and I am beginning to doubt if I can make it through this journey. I know the others are thinking this as well. But, I know General Washington means well, and if going on this perilous journey means I can be free from that menace Britain, then so be it. I will go to any lengths to make sure you and little Maisie have the best possible life. I am too far in to quit now, and I'm ready to be free.

Tell Maisie that Daddy will be home soon enough. I love you, and God bless the colonies.

Sincerely,
Richard Marshall

The Stowaway
Jacob Miller
Young Adult Division

(This is an excerpt from a larger work.)

Characters

DEATH

JONAH

Setting: Cargo hold of the cruise ship.

> (*The lighting is dim enough to indicate a storage space but light enough to see the characters (greens, blues, greys). There are cargo boxes strewn about. JONAH, the stowaway, is hidden behind a large grouping of the boxes and is not seen by the audience. DEATH is seen sitting on a box with a candle lit table in front of him and another chair opposite. DEATH's back is turned toward the area JONAH is in. There is a pizza box on the table that DEATH is eating from. DEATH is wearing a fitted grey suit with combed back hair that has noticeable amounts of gel. JONAH is wearing cargo shorts, a t-shirt, and sneakers. He appears to be in mid-20's. After several seconds, JONAH pops up and begins to look for a way out. When he spots a lone figure at the table eating pizza, he initially retreats but curiosity gets the better of him. He approaches the solitary figure, not making a sound. He does not know it is DEATH.*)

DEATH. (*Without turning around*)
Would you like something to eat?

(*Startled, Jonah stops and doesn't speak.*)

DEATH. You sure? You seem like you've been down here awhile.

(*The hunger is too much and Jonah approaches cautiously.*)

JONAH. How did you know I was here?

DEATH. I heard you breathing. (*This is a lie.*)
Either you were a person or a very large rat. And I know for a fact both like pizza.

(*By now, Jonah has begun eating with fervor. After watching him eat for a few moments,*)

What's your name, kid? (*Death already knows his name.*)

JONAH. It's Jonah. Jonah Krimp. (*Continues eating.*)

Do you have anything to drink?

DEATH. What would you like?

JONAH. Water would be great.

(*Death pulls out a bottle of water from his jacket.*)

JONAH. (*Taking the bottle, astonished.*)

Bottle of beer would be even better.

DEATH. Let's stick with the water for now.

(*Watching Jonah drink.*)

So, what're you doing down in the cargo hold?

JONAH. Oh, I'm a stowaway.

(*Pause, confusion and fear flash across his face.*)
I do not know why I told you that.

DEATH. I won't tell anyone. Besides, I fed you already. That would be cruel.

JONAH. Did you know I was here?

DEATH. What do you mean?

JONAH. Well there was a second chair here.

DEATH. (A slight smile.) Let's just say it was a coincidence.

JONAH. You're a strange person.

DEATH. Says the man who stowed away on a cruise ship.

> (*Long pause. Jonah is slightly uncomfortable. Death is enjoying it.*)

JONAH. I forgot, I never asked your name…

DEATH. (*Pause, as though Death is considering what to say.*)

Call me Tío.

> (*Tío is pronounced with a soft T, almost like a D. Tío is regarded as the Lord of the Underworld in certain places of Central America.*)

JONAH. (*Confused.*) Isn't that the Spanish word for uncle?

DEATH. (*Pleased.*) You know Spanish?

JONAH. I took a couple semesters in college.

DEATH. That would be a no then. Where did you go to school?

JONAH. Just a community college in my hometown. I dropped out after a year.

DEATH. How come?

JONAH. One morning I just woke up and didn't know what I wanted anymore.

DEATH. How'd you end up here then?

JONAH. I don't know. A week ago, I saw a flier about this cruise and immediately just left to get on it. I knew I couldn't afford it, so I just snuck on.

DEATH. (*Death stands, starts walking around.*)

It seems like you're searching for your purpose Mr. Krimp. But ships are dangerous. One bad wave can send us flying into the water. Struggling, gasping for air, trying to reach the surface. Grasping any form of hope we can latch onto. Much like your decision to drop out. Classes can be so stifling, can't they?

(*Pause.*)

We often find ourselves lost at sea. I suggest finding a life jacket.

(*The lights flash out and Death hides behind one of the boxes behind him. The lights come back on in an instant and it appears Death just vanished. Jonah is alone at the table, very confused.*)

JONAH. What the fuck…

(Lights dim out.)

END

Dragon Diaries
Finn Ross
3rd Place, Junior Division

There was a castle and there was a dragon. The castle was home to guards and knights. The dragon was a red fire breathing dragon. They lived on two sides of a deep canyon. In the canyon there was an apple tree, and there was a slide down the canyon walls so the humans could get to the apple tree.

One day a princess from the castle went down into the canyon to practice her bow and arrow shooting. The dragon saw her and swooped down. The princess shot her bow and arrow and it hurt the dragon but not too much. So the dragon flamed her bow and arrow. The princess ran from the dragon. She headed the wrong way and tried to find the castle. She was lost in the canyon and she didn't know how to rock climb.

All of the guards and knights from the castle went looking for the princess but they never ever found her. And then they thought that the dragon has taken her to his nest. When the dragon was gone playing with his dragon friend, the knights checked up in the dragon's home but they did not find the princess. The dragon's nest was a very big nest, and it was big enough across for two big dragons and one baby dragon.

When the knights checked where the girl was shooting her bow and arrows, they found only a pile of ashes and they saw her bow and arrows broken in the sand because they thought the dragon killed the princess.

The humans lit stuff on fire and shot it out at the dragon. It hit one of the dragon's wings and his tail. The dragon wasn't killed because it didn't hit his heart. But fire got on its wings. The dragon was very strong but he lost one of his wings.

Meanwhile, the princess was trying to climb the rock wall to get back to her castle. The dragon's friend saw her and helped her get back to the castle. The knights thought, "Oh! Maybe that dragon's friend helped the princess. We should help the dragon."

The dragon was very hurt and so the humans decided to help him with metal. They had a screwdriver but no screws, so they had to make screws. When they were done figuring out how to make screws they screwed the dragon's new metal wing together but it took 150 hours.

And so then the dragons wrote a letter to the humans that said, "thank you for helping." The dragons didn't really know how to write so they just did scribbles but the humans understood it. And so they were happy that they helped the dragons and they became friends from that moment on.

Tweety's Diary
Lillian Ross
2nd Place, Junior Division

July 1, 2021

Dear Diary,

My name is Tweety and I just turned 18 days. You might be thinking, "Tweety is a weird name for a human." But actually, I'm not a human. I am a bird! I am a female goldfinch. And you must be wondering, "how can a bird have a diary?" Here's how it all happened: my mother was flying when she spotted a human pretending to read this diary. And then she swooped down and grabbed it straight out of the human's hands. And my mother says the human shrieked in a squeaky voice, "YOU GET BACK HERE BIRD! THAT'S NOT YOUR DIARY! THAT'S MINE! I WILL NOT GIVE UP UNTIL I HAVE IT!" That's what she said, and don't you want to laugh? I just want to laugh at the human's squeaky shrieking voice.

I just turned 18 days and my mother says I'm getting too big to live in this nest. So tomorrow I am going to move out of my nest and I'm going to find a mate. I hope my mate and I will have some eggs and raise some cute chicks together.

July 2, 2021

Dear Diary,

Here I am out of my mother's nest. Now all I need to do is find a mate, then build a nest, and have some baby eggs.

This morning, when I was flying, I spotted the human whose diary my mom stole! She was very angry, and she was even begging her parents to buy her a new diary in the squeakiest voice possible.

She said, "Mom, Dad, buy me a new diary! A bird took my old one!!"

Her parents said, "honey, a bird can't steal your old diary. Now please show me where your old diary is hidden."

And then the girl said angrily "You don't believe me! Let's go in the house!" And then they walked in the giant nest that humans call a house. I flew away trying to find a good spot to build a nest.

I kept flying until I found the perfect Elm tree to build a nest in the garden. The garden was like a buffet for goldfinches. It had so many aster, thistle, and sunflower plants. Now I just need a mate to agree that I found the perfect nesting spot!

Guess who was behind me the whole time I was flying around looking for the perfect nesting spot? Five male goldfinches about my age, and they kept chasing me and begging for me to mate them! They even said I was the prettiest female goldfinch they had ever seen! Alas, I can only mate one of them so I agreed to try a date with each of them to see if I like them. Tonight, I'm going on a flight with one of them and seeing if I like him.

Later

I just got back from my flight with one of the male goldfinches. Ick!!! He didn't know how to do any acrobatics. And his song was horrible! It reminded me of that squeaky girl. Well, the next one up is a different bird so I'm hoping that he'll be better than the first one.

Later Still

I just got back from my flight with the second goldfinch and it was worse than the first. His song was deep with squeaky notes and I hated flying with him. He kept begging me to mate with him even though we hadn't built our nest together yet! Well, I am too tired to go out on another flight tonight so I think I might take a break from finding a mate and sleep.

July 3, 2021

Good morning, dear Diary.

I had a lovely song last night. Did you know birds can sing while they're sleeping? Based on my internal clock it is about 4:00 in the morning. Time to sing my dawn chorus! I love to fly around singing at dawn because I'm bursting with energy and it feels good to get it out.

The third male goldfinch that I'm going out with is awake now, and he is very pretty. The golden feathers on his breast are super bright and his song is lovely. But I'm still questioning his acrobatics. He won't show them to me. He says we better wait until our time to fly. So I have no idea what his acrobatic skills are. I like to do flips in the air and twirls, and I am attracted to males who like doing those things, too. I better go off and fly with him to see if he likes what I like.

Later

I just got back and the third goldfinch is HORRIBLE at acrobatics! He only liked doing tricks on tree branches and thistles. He hated doing flips while he's flying. He hated flying. Can you believe that?

My flights with the first three goldfinch mates weren't that great. I hope the flights with the fourth and fifth goldfinch suitors are better than the first, second, and third. I can see the fourth goldfinch and I'm noticing now that his feathers are a little bit prettier than the third. His upper parts and lower parts are a bright lemon yellow with no streaks of brown. Same with the fifth goldfinch! Let's hope they like acrobatics. See ya when I get back!

Still Later

I just got back from my flight with the fourth goldfinch. He liked flying a little bit more than the third, and he only liked doing tumble-y things in the air. I had no idea how to do the tumble-y things! And I would like a mate that knows how to do the same things as me, and that I know how to do the same things as him! Now it's time for my flight with the fifth.

Even Later

I JUST FOUND THE PERFECT MATE! The fifth goldfinch, William, loves doing the things that I do. He knows so many silly jokes. His feathers are a perfect goldfinch color – a goldy-yellow. And he loves all the things that I love. He has the perfect song! I am going to show him the place where I picked out the perfect spot for our nest.

July 11, 2021

Dear Diary,

It's been a few days since I've written because I've been busy building a nest. And the best part is William agreed with me that the spot in the Elm Tree that I picked out is the perfect spot for a nest. First, I collected root fibers and other sticks. Then I tied it to the branches of the Elm tree with spider silk. I used the fluffy pappus material from the plants that I like to eat like the sunflower, aster, and thistle plants. It took me 6 whole days to finish! I'm really going to need a nap!

We had a little vacation and we mated. When we got back to our nest, I laid four beautiful little pale blue eggs. I hope I am all prepared to become a mother.

July 24, 2021

Dear Diary,

Today is a super-duper special day. My eggs are hatching! I think Penny just pipped through... aww! You can do it, Penny! Elizabeth has already hatched, so has Harry. Henry and Penny are the last hatchlings to get out of their eggs. Oh! It looks like Henry just pipped through. Aww! You can do it, Henry! Penny is already out of her egg. I think she might know karate! It's taking Henry a really long time.

Later

Henry has finally gotten out of his egg! My four little chicks are here! Look at how cute each one of them are! They look so helpless and they have the cutest little wisps of grey down.

William's job is to feed the chicks and me. William is going to get some thistle and aster seeds. He should be back soon.

July 25, 2021

Dear Diary,

I stayed awake all night. I guess having chicks is way harder than I thought. I thought they were supposed to just sit around and be cute and snuggle me – but they're not. Instead they are chirpy and constantly looking for food. My chicks are so cute. I'm probably going to say that a lot. Because they are super-duper cute.

Elizabeth and Penny are best friends. We call Elizabeth Liz for short. So Liz and Penny are best friends. Same with Harry and Henry. They're playing together all in harmony. Now that they're not bothering me, I think I might take a 1-hour long nap. Goodnight Diary.

August 8, 2021

Dear Diary,

My chicks are starting to fly! William and I are so excited that our chicks are learning to fly. I can't wait for them to finally learn how to fly! It's taking a lot of hard work.

Okay, all of my chicks are up here so now I am going to do a head count. One, two, three, WAIT. Where's the fourth one? Liz is missing! She must have fallen from the nest! I better go find her. Sorry, Diary, I'm too busy to write much.

Later

I went flying over the yard that we nested in and spotted Liz on the ground. I sat in a nearby sapling to calm her down. Then, the humans came by and spotted Liz, and they put her in a shoebox with some nice but weird snuggly and warm stuff. I have no idea what it's called. They placed the shoebox in the branches of a nearby tree. I picked her up and brought her back to our home. I am so relieved that my baby is back in the nest!

August 9, 2021

Dear Diary,

My chicks are so beautiful and so grown up! Why couldn't they have stayed chicks forever? Although they don't wake me up anymore, so that's a positive thing.

They're so great. Even Liz has learned how to fly perfectly, and she doesn't even fall on the ground anymore! I'm going to miss them so much when they finally fly away. Now they have beautiful feathers, and I can easily tell which is male and which is female by the coloring of their feathers. Well, I love my chicks as much as any mother bird would, and I am going to be super sad when the day comes that my chicks fly away.

August 11, 2021

Dear Diary,

Today is the day when my chicks fly away. Luckily, I'm already incubating my next brood! I'll be so sad when the first batch flies away.

I have one little gift to give my girls before Liz and Penny leave. I'm going to say, "Liz and Penny, you are some beautiful chicks and I am so proud to be your mother. I hope that you take good care of this diary. Don't let that squeaky human catch you with this!"

I imagine that they will say, "Thank you mom! This is going to be one of our treasured possessions. We'll write in it each day and we'll make sure our chicks have some room to write in it, and their chicks, and on and on and on. It will be nice for their chicks to know who their ancestors were through this diary."

The End

Alone Together
Christine Webb
1st Place, Adult Division

Sad news doesn't usually arrive in a metallic purple envelope.

While holding the stack of mail from my mailbox, I put the purple envelope on top. It will cover up the past-due notices. Then I see the return address, and I put it back at the bottom. I'd rather read the bills.

The welcome mat by my apartment door faded years ago, sort of like the welcome itself. People rarely visit apartment 321B.

Once inside, I throw all the mail on the kitchen table. My dog starts barking from the bedroom. "Stop it, Dragon!" I yell. "I'll be there in a minute."

I didn't name my dog Dragon. That was her name at the shelter. I tried to rename her Ms. Fluff. She's a small spaniel/terrier mix with droopy ears and huge eyes. After Ms. Fluff, I tried to name her Paisley. Then Lady. Then Doggie (I was getting desperate). Every time, she stared blankly at me until I called her Dragon, and then she'd smile with her tongue out and wag her tail so hard that her whole back end wagged. Dragon is a ridiculous name, but she won't accept anything else.

Once the oven is on preheat for my lasagna-for-one, I take Dragon out for a walk in the crisp September air. The mail is still unopened on my counter, and I'm trying to forget about it. Dragon's furry brown ears bounce as she runs to chase every bug on the sidewalk. She eats an ant, looks back at the ground, then looks at me as if to say, "Hey, where did it go?"

By the time I convince myself to open the purple envelope, the lasagna dishes are in the sink and Dragon is chewing a bone. Reality TV lights up the darkening living room.

The envelope contains an invitation to a baby shower. Tiny purple elephants march across a pink background, and my sister's name is scrawled across the front. She would never design an invitation like this - I bet my mom did it. Even though I figured something like this would happen one day, knowing that I'm not there for it puts cement in my stomach. Their lives have simply...gone on. Without me.

My sister has written on the back of the invitation in her no-nonsense, black-ink cursive: "You probably won't come, but I thought you might want to know. It's a girl. Due November 23."

When we were little, she tried to teach me how to write in cursive like that. We played school all the time – she was the teacher. The only time I got to be the teacher, I declared we were playing "med school" and did surgery on one of her teddy bears. He didn't make it.

If we were still speaking, I'd buy a doctor teddy bear for her baby. That story has been told so many times that my whole family would get the joke. We'd smile and laugh and talk about the good old days. But some things, like a bear with stuffing in every corner of the living room, can't be put back together.

I missed my sister's wedding for a medical school interview at my dream school. That was the last straw on a pile of growing resentments. She yelled that I was so selfish, I cried that she was incredibly vain...we both said a lot of things we shouldn't have said. They don't matter now.

Also, in the end, I didn't even get into medical school.

The invitation blurs as I throw it away, and I attempt to get lost in watching made-for-TV love. Dragon jumps up on the couch and cuddles close, like she knows something's wrong.

A knock on the door startles me. Dragon's brown eyebrows furrow, and she jumps off the couch like she's ready to attack. She attempts a growl, but it's far from menacing. If a serial killer wants to take me down, Dragon will be no help.

When I look through the peephole, the giant eyeball of a man who is also staring through the peephole is looking back at me. I back up, feeling for a moment that he can see me too.

Against my better judgement, I crack open the door. "Can I help you?"

"Are you Mel?" he asks.

"Yes." I should have said no. What if he's a debt collector?

"My name is Jax," he says. "Can I come in?"

I'm about to close the door, but a dog nose nudges inside through the crack. Debt collectors don't usually bring dogs with them. I don't think serial killers do either, though I've had less experience with those.

I open the door wide enough for Jax and his dog to come in. Jax is a tall, lanky man, probably mid-twenties, with shaggy blonde hair and square-rimmed glasses. He's wearing a mustard-yellow turtleneck, and his black shorts match his ratty black briefcase. His Birkenstock knockoffs are green.

"Heck yeah!" he says as soon as he sees Dragon. "It is you!" He throws his briefcase on my couch to free up both hands for petting her.

Dragon and the man's dog start sniffing each other. The other dog is a little bit larger than Dragon, but their coloring and features are similar.

Jax smiles and sighs while he scratches the scruff of Dragon's neck. "Do you think they remember each other?"

My eyebrows shoot up. "Should they?"

He stands up. "Oh right. You don't know." His eyes dart around. "You may want to sit down." He gestures to the couch, like he's the host who just invited me in instead of the other way around.

He sits with his briefcase in his lap and rustles through it, trying to locate the correct paperwork. Meanwhile, his dog has taken Dragon's bone and started chewing it. Dragon tilts her head, confused by this turn of events.

"Three years ago," Jax starts dramatically, "You went to the Shiawassee Humane Society. You were looking for a friend, a companion. A furry little someone to keep you warm at night. Someone to talk to about life's troubles. A creature who could show you the unconditional love that all of us so desperately need." He gazes out the window, lost in thought.

"Uh huh," I nudge. "I did go to the humane society, and that's where I got Dragon..."

"Yes, Draaaggon." He drags the word out thoughtfully like it's the answer to some long-forgotten puzzle. "I saw her name on the paperwork. Interesting choice."

"I didn't choose it."

"Of course, you didn't." He looks at me like I'm an idiot for suggesting otherwise. "The Glenfelds of Milwaukee did. They're huge D&D fans. Their son presented at ComicCon last month. Great kid." He shakes his head and laughs at some unexplained memory.

"I see," I say, even though I don't.

"When the Glenfelds moved out of state, they couldn't take Dragon with them. Something about allergies or the new house being haunted or something. Which is how she ended up at the Shiawassee Humane Society, which is how she ended up here. Anyway," he shuffles through some papers in his briefcase again before pulling one out, "I have some news."

I brace myself, but I'm not quite sure for what.

"I've been doing ancestry work on Zipper." He nods to the dog chewing on Dragon's bone, and the dog looks up at the mention of his name. The bone hangs out of his mouth like a giant cigar. "I've discovered something quite serious. Zipper has…" his voice catches, and he takes a moment to compose himself. "He has an elevated risk of contracting Syringomyelia." He closes his eyes and puts his fist in front of his mouth as if even saying the words have hurt him. Then he puts his hand on the couch near me, as if reaching out in comfort. "We have to be strong."

I blink at him.

His eyes are full of compassion, as if I'm going to break down at any moment. I say the first thing that comes to mind. "Dog ancestry?"

Jax looks flustered, like I didn't react correctly. "Yes. I bought the DNA test kit. The results, obviously, were devastating. I've been on a quest to warn all of Zipper's relatives. My search has taken me to three and a half states. There's a chance that one of his siblings was transferred to Germany with a military family, but I haven't been able to go there yet. I've started a GoFundMe." He purses his lips. "It hasn't received much traction."

"That's too bad." I do my best to look appalled. "So what is this Syringo…thing?"

"Syringomyelia. Fluid develops near the spinal cord." He shoots a glance at Zipper and drops his voice to a whisper. "It can cause extreme neck and back pain."

"Is it fatal?" My pulse quickens. Dragon may be a goof, but she's all I've got.

Jax rolls his eyes like I'm missing the point. "It's not usually fatal, but would you like to have extreme neck and back pain? Would you, Mel?"

"No."

"Okay then." He nods like that settles it. "Here." He pulls an envelope out of his briefcase. "It's an invitation to Zipper's family reunion. It's also going to double as a support group for those of us dealing with the looming threat of this debilitating disease." He puts his hand on his heart.

The invitation is typed up on a regular-sized piece of computer paper. The reunion is being held about an hour away from here at a park. A giant picture of Zipper takes up half the page, and there's a small graphic of something medical (a spine?) in the bottom corner. It's probably related to this might-one-day-happen-maybe genetic disease.

"Just look at them," says Jax, smiling at the dogs. "Back together after all this time."

Dragon is looking at me, eyes wide, as if pleading with me to get her bone back from Zipper. I pull another one off the shelf and give it to her. She trots over, lies down next to Zipper, and the sounds of contented gnawing fill the room.

"I'm not sure they recognize each other," I say, "but they seem happy enough."

"I bet they remember." Jax leans forward, watching them. "Don't you feel like on some level, family always stays connected?"

A chill darts through me. "No, I don't think so."

"Really?" He looks shocked. "But it's family." He says it like perhaps I misheard him the first time.

Jax's quirkiness feels annoying now, and I cross my arms. "They're just dogs."

Jax gasps and scoops up Zipper. Zipper's so startled that he drops his bone, and his face droops. Jax holds Zipper up like he's burping a baby and pats his back. "There, there," he whispers. "She didn't mean it."

Perhaps I would have rather had a debt collector at my door. This guy is cuckoo.

He turns back to me, still bouncing his dog. "Why can't family stay connected?"

"They should," I say. My chest tightens. "In a perfect world, that would be great. It doesn't always work out that way."

"I see," says Jax, even though he doesn't.

His bouncing slows, and he puts Zipper back down. Zipper runs over and picks up the bone, resuming his chewing position near Dragon.

Jax sits back on the couch, and there's a thick silence. "I never had a family," he finally says.

"Oh?" It's a syllable of politeness rather than interest.

"I was in foster care, thrown from house to house, until I was eighteen. After I aged out, I got a job at a grocery store. Worked all the way up to assistant manager of the night shift." He pulls his badge out of his briefcase and flashes it like he's proving that he's in the FBI.

"Wow." Another one-syllable response. Not sure if I'm hoping he'll leave or keep talking. It's a little of both.

"Anyway, I've always wished I had a family. Christmas dinner and birthday cake and a crazy uncle, you know? The whole thing. But I don't. It's just me and Zipper." He picks up the invitation, looks at the picture, and smiles.

Not for the first time, I wonder if a difficult family past is better or worse than none at all. "In some ways, no family makes things less complicated."

"Maybe." He shrugs like he doesn't mean it. "I wanted something more for Zipper. He deserves the chance to know where he came from, to get back together with the dogs who loved him. We all deserve that, right? But dogs are easier than people. Sometimes when you find people, they don't want you back." He looks to the floor, his mouth tight.

"Sometimes." I swallow. What would they do if I came back? Is it better to wonder or to find out a truth that I wish I hadn't?

Jax is leaning forward on the couch, scrutinizing the dogs like they're a science experiment. "Deep down," he says, "Really really deep down – don't you think a piece of them still feels connected? Maybe it's just buried deep?" His turns his head, meeting my eyes. He looks sad and thoughtful, like he's begging me to agree with him. He seems small, suddenly much younger than he is.

Dragon licks Zipper's ear.

"I don't know," I say. "Maybe. Hard to tell."

"Yeah, that's what I've been thinking too." He rubs his hands on his shorts. We watch the dogs again. Maybe Jax isn't so bad.

"Do you want a drink?" I ask. "You can stay a while if you want. The dogs can play."

"Sure," he says. He heads toward the kitchen. "They might as well enjoy the good years they have left before their spines betray them."

The kitchen is a mess, but Jax doesn't seem to care. "What do you want to drink?" I ask, searching my cupboards. "Water, milk that expired last week, or powdered lemonade? Oh, here's a hot cocoa from last winter."

"I'll take the lemonade," he says. He takes the container out of my hands and starts opening drawers, looking for a spoon. I decide on the hot cocoa. When I rip the top off the packet, I pause over the garbage can.

I reach down with the other hand and pull out the purple envelope.

Acknowledgements

The Vicksburg Cultural Arts Center would like to thank all of the judges, coaches and volunteers who helped bring this program to life in 2021. We could not have done it without you!

This program has been made possible in part with support from the Irving S. Gilmore Foundation, the Vicksburg Foundation and Meijer.

For more information about the Tournament of Writers, visit the Vicksburg Cultural Arts Center's website at
www.vicksburgarts.com/tournament-of-writers

Made in the USA
Coppell, TX
02 September 2021